GROUP'S
DINNER
A AND MOVIE

Friendship, Faith, and Fun for **All Ages**

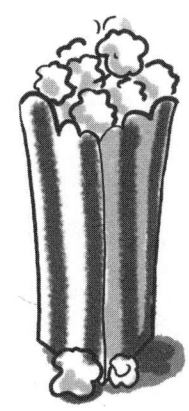

Loveland, Colorado

www.group.com

Group resources actually work!

This Group resource incorporates our R.E.A.L. approach to ministry. It reinforces a growing friendship with Jesus, encourages long-term learning, and results in life transformation, because it's

Relational
Learner-to-learner interaction enhances learning and builds Christian friendships.

Experiential
What learners experience through discussion and action sticks with them up to 9 times longer than what they simply hear or read.

Applicable
The aim of Christian education is to equip learners to be both hearers and doers of God's Word.

Learner-based
Learners understand and retain more when the learning process takes into consideration how they learn best.

Group's Dinner and a Movie: G-Rated
Copyright © 2008 Group Publishing, Inc.

All rights reserved. No part of this book may be reproduced in any manner whatsoever without prior written permission from the publisher, except where noted in the text and in the case of brief quotations embodied in critical articles and reviews. For information, e-mail Permissions at inforights@group.com, or write Permissions, Group Publishing, Inc., Ministry Essentials, P.O. Box 481, Loveland, CO 80539.

Visit our Web site: **group.com**

Credits
Contributing Authors: Linda Crawford, Heather Dunn, Gina Leuthauser, Mike Van Schooneveld, Jill Wuellner
Editor: Ann Marie Rozum
Senior Developer: Amy Nappa
Project Manager: Scott M. Kinner
Chief Creative Officer: Joani Schultz
Copy Editor: Dena Twinem
Art Director: Andrea Filer
Print Production Artist: YaYe Design
Illustrator: Alan Flinn
Production Manager: Peggy Naylor

Unless otherwise noted, Scripture taken from the HOLY BIBLE, NEW INTERNATIONAL VERSION®. Copyright © 1973, 1978, 1984 by International Bible Society. Used by permission of Zondervan Publishing House. All rights reserved.

Library of Congress Cataloging-in-Publication Data

Group's dinner and a movie : G-rated : friendship, faith, and fun for
all ages / [contributing authors, Linda Crawford ... et al.]. -- 1st
American pbk. ed.
  p. cm.
 ISBN 978-0-7644-3661-1 (pbk. : alk. paper) 1. Church group work. 2.
Motion pictures in church work. 3. Cookery--Religious
aspects--Christianity. I. Crawford, Linda, 1938-
 BV652.2.G693 2008
 253'.7--dc22
                        2007038350

ISBN 978-0-7644-3661-1

Printed in the United States of America.
10 9 8 7 6 5 4 3 2   17 16 15 14 13 12 11 10 09 08

Friendship, Faith, and Fun for All Ages

TABLE OF CONTENTS

Introduction 4

Finding Nemo 5

Chicken Run 12

Mary Poppins 19

Willy Wonka and the Chocolate Factory 26

The Sound of Music 33

Charlotte's Web 41

The Wizard of Oz 48

Cars 56

Swiss Family Robinson 64

The Rookie 72

Meet the Robinsons 78

101 Dalmatians 85

Invitations 93

3

INTRODUCTION

Welcome to *Group's Dinner and a Movie: G-Rated*, a resource for people of all ages who really love food and movies!

During these out-of-the-ordinary small-group events, you'll cook a meal together with your friends and families, and you'll enjoy lively discussion around the dinner table (TalkStarters are included with each event). Then you'll watch a movie together and enjoy some really great snacks. Afterward you'll discuss the spiritual themes of the movie.

Cooking and sharing meals together will really increase the dynamics of the fellowship in your group of friends and families. As you chop, stir, cook, eat, and laugh together, you'll learn about one another and build memories that will last a lifetime. It's easy to include children in your cooking with the Cooking Together tips. You'll learn to be a community. Isn't that just what God wants for your church?

Not only that, there's much to learn about ourselves and God in the movies. We'll see disobedience, betrayal, regret, and revenge. We'll also see love, sacrifice, grace, and redemption. All of these themes, played out in a variety of family-friendly comedies and adventure stories, can powerfully teach all ages about the God we serve and how to follow him more. Besides that, watching these movies with an eye toward the spiritual will help families look for God in every movie or TV show they watch.

These events are great anytime. They're perfect to use for a family night or small-group gathering. You can have a Dinner and a Movie once a quarter, once a month, or anytime families or small groups want to get together for something out of the ordinary.

We hope you enjoy these Dinner and a Movie events! Start the show!

IS IT LEGAL TO SHOW THESE MOVIES TO MY SMALL GROUP?

In general, federal copyright laws do allow you to use videos or DVDs for the purpose of home viewing as long as you aren't charging admission. However, you may feel more comfortable if you purchase a license. Your church can obtain a license from Christian Video Licensing International for a small fee. Just visit www.cvli.org or call 1-888-302-6020 for more information. When using a movie that is not covered by the license, we recommend directly contacting the production company to seek permission to use it.

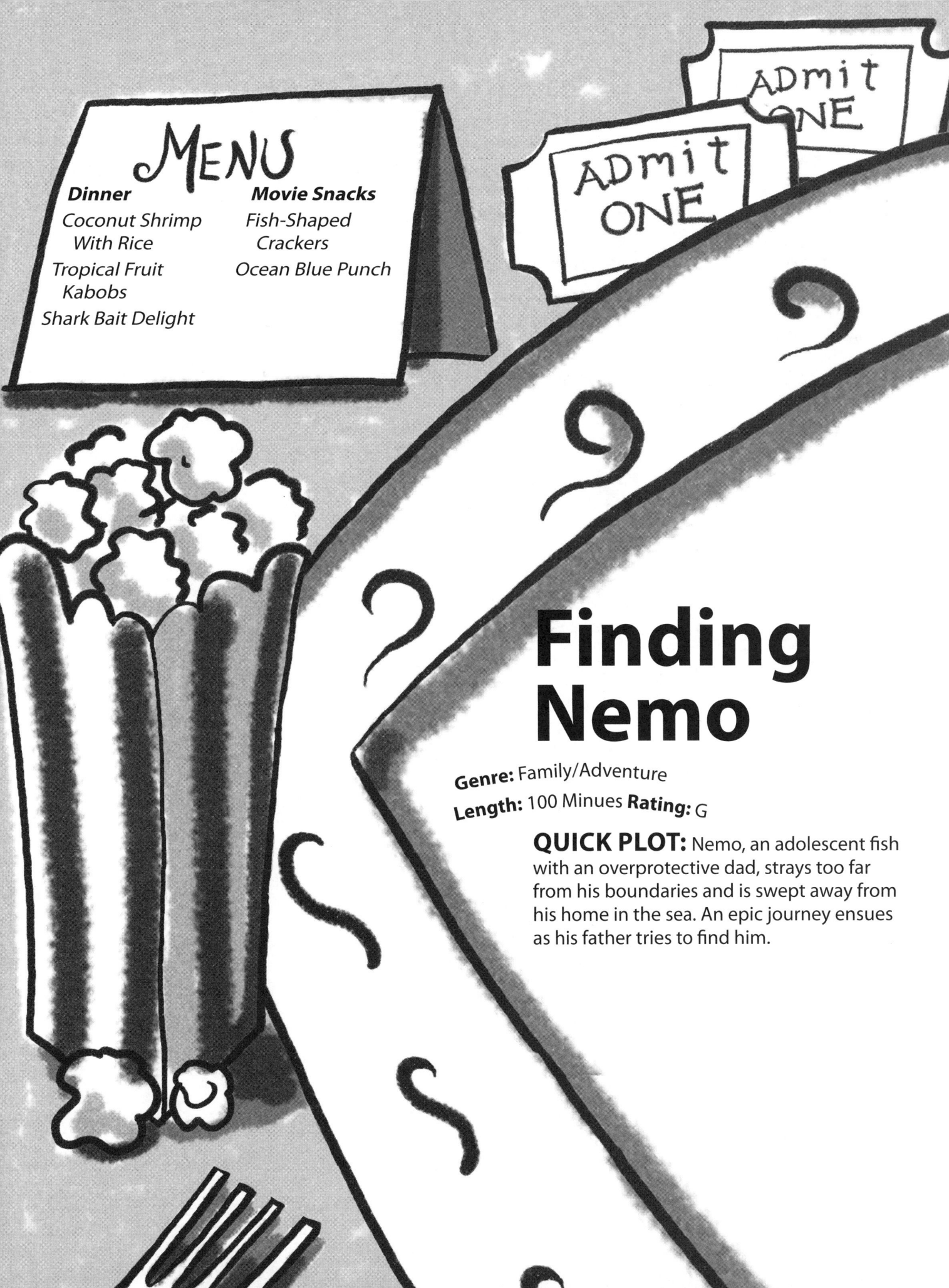

Easy Option Meal

Save time on meal preparation by serving Piggyback Fish Sticks (goldfish crackers stuck to the top of fish sticks with tarter sauce) along with pre-sliced tropical fruits such as pineapple and mango from your grocery store's deli. Finish off with Nemo-colored orange sherbet or orange cream Popsicle flavored ices. Of course, you could avoid kitchen time altogether by picking up fish and chips from a local fast-food restaurant.

TIP:

You can find coconut milk in the Asian section of your grocery store, or ask an employee to help you find it. And you don't have to use light—it just makes the dish a bit less heavy.

Permission to photocopy this page from *Group's Dinner and a Movie: G-Rated* granted for local church use. Copyright © Group Publishing, Inc., P.O. Box 481, Loveland, CO 80539. www.group.com.

SUPPLIES

Before your Dinner and a Movie event, you may want to talk to everyone who plans to attend and divide up the ingredients list. Keep in mind that some items may cost a lot more than others. Perhaps two people would like to share the cost of those ingredients, while others each bring a couple of items.

What you'll need: / **Names:**

Coconut Shrimp With Rice (serves 8)
- 2 cups rice
- 2 pounds medium shrimp, peeled and deveined
- 3 tablespoons olive oil
- 1½ onions
- 3 cloves of garlic
- 2 teaspoons fresh ginger
- 1 teaspoon cilantro
- ¼ teaspoon cumin
- 2 cups light coconut milk
- 2 teaspoons sugar
- ¼ teaspoon red pepper flakes
- salt

Tropical Fruit Kabobs (serves 8)
- 2 star fruits
- 6 medium bananas
- 10 medium kiwis
- one 20-ounce can pineapple chunks
- bamboo skewers

Ocean Blue Punch (makes 3 quarts)
- 1 packet blue raspberry powdered drink mix
- sugar (according to powdered drink mix directions)
- one 10-ounce can frozen pineapple juice, thawed
- 1 liter ginger ale

Extras
Fish-shaped cheese crackers for a movie snack

Make Ahead **Shark Bait Delight (recipe on page 8)**

COCONUT SHRIMP WITH RICE

- 2 cups rice
- 2 pounds medium shrimp, peeled and deveined (can substitute chicken)
- 3 tablespoons olive oil
- 1½ onions, chopped
- 3 cloves of garlic, minced
- 2 teaspoons fresh ginger, grated
- 1 teaspoon cilantro
- ¼ teaspoon cumin
- 2 cups light coconut milk
- 2 teaspoons sugar
- ¼ teaspoon red pepper flakes
- salt to taste

Prepare rice according to package directions. (For a fun surprise, add a drop or two of blue food coloring to the water to make "ocean rice.") Heat oil in a large skillet over medium heat. Add the shrimp and cook for 5 minutes. Remove shrimp to a plate, and set aside. Add the onion, garlic, ginger, cilantro, and cumin, and cook until onion is tender. Stir in coconut milk, sugar, and red pepper, and bring to a simmer. Add the shrimp, cover, and cook for 10 minutes. Salt to taste. Serve over rice. Serves 8.

TIP:

If you have picky kids, substitute chicken breast tenders for the shrimp in this recipe.

TROPICAL FRUIT KABOBS

- 2 star fruits
- 6 medium bananas, cut into 1-inch pieces
- 10 medium kiwis, peeled and quartered
- one 20-ounce can pineapple chunks
- bamboo skewers

Have the adults slice star fruits into ½-inch slices (so they resemble stars). Cut bananas and kiwis into bite-sized pieces.

Have the kids (aided by an adult) thread the fruit onto skewers, alternating fruits. Serves 8.

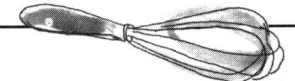

OCEAN BLUE PUNCH

- 1 packet blue raspberry powdered drink mix
- water (according to powdered drink directions)
- sugar (according to powdered drink directions)
- one 10-ounce can frozen pineapple juice, thawed
- 1 liter ginger ale

Mix powdered drink with sugar and water in a punch bowl, according to package directions. Add pineapple juice and ginger ale. Makes 3 quarts.

TIP:

Add "Nemo" to the Ocean Blue Punch by including a large scoop of orange sherbet.

GROUP'S DINNER AND A MOVIE: G-RATED

Set the Stage

Create an underwater paradise for your movie night. Drape the walls or floor with blue sheets. Hang blue or green streamer paper in front of the door to create an entry to your ocean room. Create simple fish cut outs in bright colors such as orange, red, yellow, and blue. Punch a hole in the top and hang them from the ceiling.

Make an undersea centerpiece by filling a fishbowl with colorful marbles or pebbles and adding aquarium items such as treasure chests and artificial seaweed. Better yet: Do you happen to own a gold fish?

As guests arrive, give each a small bottle of bubble solution to create a bubbly underwater atmosphere. Play a bit of island music, and you're ready for an ocean party!

Make Ahead

SHARK BAIT DELIGHT

2 cups boiling water
one 8-serving package blue gelatin
2 cups cold water
jelly beans
gummy sharks
2 cups whipped topping

Layer jelly beans on the bottom of a 9x13-inch pan to resemble sand. In a large bowl, combine gelatin powder with boiling water. Stir until completely dissolved. Stir in cold water, and pour into the 9x13-inch pan. Refrigerate for 45 minutes. Before the gelatin sets, add gummy sharks to the mixture. Before serving, top with whipped topping. Apply whipped topping with a spatula, peaking it slightly to look like the crests of waves. Serves 10-12.

COOKING TOGETHER

1. Make the Shark Bait Delight according to the recipe above before your guests arrive.

2. Shortly before your guests arrive, begin the rice for the Coconut Shrimp with Rice as it can take 30 minutes to cook.

3. When everyone arrives, have two volunteers make the Ocean Blue Punch according to the recipe on page 7.

4. Have two people working on the Coconut Shrimp according to the recipe on page 7. One person can cut the onion, while the other gets all the ingredients and spices ready. Then they can start cooking!

5. Have a volunteer cut up fruit for the Tropical Fruit Kabobs. Remind kids of the importance of washing their hands before preparing food, then have other volunteers supervise kids as they thread the fruit onto skewers. It's a good idea for adults to hold the skewers as kids push fruit onto them.

Permission to photocopy this page from *Group's Dinner and a Movie: G-Rated* granted for local church use.
Copyright © Group Publishing, Inc., P.O. Box 481, Loveland, CO 80539. www.group.com.

6. Have one person create "waves" on the Shark Bait Delight using a spatula and whipped topping.

7. Remaining volunteers can set the table and prepare beverages.

8. When everything is ready, move the food to your serving table, and ask someone to pray over your meal.

9. After eating, make cleanup easy by inviting everyone to pitch in. Then set out fish-shaped crackers and Ocean Blue Punch for your guests and get ready for the movie!

> **Meal Time TalkStarters**
> - *If you could live in the sea, what kind of fish or sea creature would you like to be? Why?*
> - *Have you ever gotten lost? What happened?*
> - *Has anyone ever gone out of his or her way to help you? How?*
> - *Tell about any peculiar fears or phobias you have.*

LET'S WATCH A MOVIE!
FINDING NEMO

THE PRE-SHOW

Have everyone gather in the area where you'll show the movie. If you've just finished eating dinner together, you may want to provide a quick break for people to use the restroom.

When everyone is together, serve fish crackers to anyone who wants snacks. Be sure to provide napkins (a tropical motif would be fun).

Have adults team up with kids in groups of three to five, and give each group a piece of paper and pen. Ask groups to answer these trivia questions about fish. Then read the answers aloud so all can compare their answers to the correct ones.

BIG FISH, LITTLE FISH TRIVIA QUIZ

1. Which is longer, a whale shark or a killer whale?
2. How many teeth does a blue shark have in its lifetime?
3. What structure made of living sea creatures can be seen from outer space?
4. About how long can a sea turtle live?
5. How big is the largest aquarium?

Answers

1. A whale shark. Though killer whales can grow as long as 32 feet, the whale shark is the longest fish, often reaching 45 feet!
2. Sharks replace their teeth every six to eight weeks, so a shark probably goes through thousands of teeth in its lifetime.
3. The Great Barrier Reef in Australia.
4. They've been known to live over 80 years!
5. The Georgia Aquarium needs 8 million gallons of water to support over 100,000 fish and animals. It probably wouldn't fit in your living room.

THE SHOW
Finding Nemo

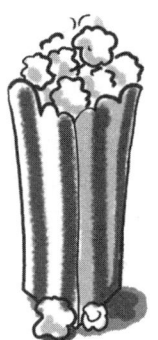

Genre: Family/Adventure

Length: 100 Minutes

Rating: G (Some scenes may be frightening to little ones, such as a barracuda attacking the reef in the opening scene, and a shark chasing Marlin and Dory when it smells blood.)

Plot: Set in Australia's Great Barrier Reef, *Finding Nemo* is about a clownfish, Marlin, who loves his son, Nemo, but his overprotective parenting begins to strain their relationship. In an act of rebellion, Nemo swims in a forbidden area and gets caught by divers who take him far away from the reef.

Marlin tries desperately to follow the boat where Nemo is captive, but he can't swim fast enough and no one will help him—until he encounters a talkative, forgetful blue tang fish named Dory. Marlin doesn't really take Dory seriously (who would?) and has a hard time trusting her. In fact, it's his constant fear and mistrust of everyone that causes Marlin to fall into trouble throughout his journey.

As he finally begins to take chances and make new friends, Marlin realizes that he may have been unfair to his son. Meanwhile, with the help of his own new friends in a dentist's aquarium where he's "imprisoned," Nemo discovers bravery that he didn't know he had.

THE POST-SHOW

After the movie, use some or all of these questions to discuss the spiritual themes in *Finding Nemo*.

 Which character are you most like, and why?

 What advice would you give Marlin about being a good parent? What advice would you give Nemo about being a good son?

 By the end of the movie, Marlin has overcome his distrust of others and his fear of the ocean. What fear have you overcome? How did you do that?

 At first, Marlin ignored Dory and wouldn't listen to her because he thought she was weird and different. Have you ever done this to someone? If so, what do you think you missed out on?

 It was hard for Marlin to trust Dory. What do you think it takes to trust someone?

 Nemo lacked confidence because one of his fins was weaker than the other. In what area do you wish you had more confidence? What can you do about that?

 As you watched *Finding Nemo*, what did you learn about God's undersea creation that you didn't know before?

 How is Marlin's relationship with Nemo like God's relationship with us? How is it different?

Bible Passages

You may want to use these Bible passages during your movie discussion:

- *Matthew 18:12-14*—The parable of the lost sheep.
- *Ephesians 6:1-4*—Honor your family.
- *2 Thessalonians 2:16-17*—God encourages us.

PRAYER

End the evening by praying together. Thank God that, like Marlin trying to find Nemo, he never gives up on us and always loves us.

SUPPLIES

Before your Dinner and a Movie event, you may want to talk to everyone in the group and divide the ingredients list. Keep in mind that some items, such as the chicken, cost more than others. Perhaps two people would like to share the cost of the meat, while others each bring a couple of items.

What you'll need:	Names:
Mrs. Tweedy's Homemade Chicken Pie (serves 6)	
1 frozen pie crust	_____
½ cup onion	_____
½ cup mushrooms	_____
1 cup frozen peas	_____
1 cup frozen chopped carrots	_____
3 tablespoons butter	_____
⅓ cup flour	_____
½ teaspoon salt	_____
½ teaspoon dried thyme	_____
¼ teaspoon pepper	_____
2 cups chicken broth	_____
¾ cup milk	_____
Meat from 2 medium deli-roasted chickens (preferably removed from bones ahead of time)	_____
Dirt and Worms (serves 8-10) two 4-serving size packages chocolate pudding mix	_____
2 cups milk	_____
1½ cups whipped topping	_____
one 20-ounce package chocolate sandwich cookies	_____
gummy worms	_____
Extras beverages	_____
microwave popcorn	_____
Make Ahead **Chive Mashers (recipe on page 14)**	_____

Easy Option Meal

Buy frozen chicken potpies or a bucket of fried chicken to simplify your menu. Accompany with deli side dishes such as mashed potatoes and corn, and warm up a frozen apple pie—and you're done!

Set the Stage

Create an atmosphere of dinner on a quaint chicken farm by using lots of red and white gingham along with denim (a red and white checkered paper tablecloth from a party supply store would be perfect, for example). For a special touch, you could even hang an indoor clothesline with denim jeans and work shirts.

Use your imagination and a black marker to make fun, rustic-looking signs from corrugated cardboard. For example, your TV room could be labeled "chicken coop" and the dining area "feedlot." Place egg cartons and homemade nests made from raffia or shredded packaging material throughout your meeting areas, and fill these with plastic or hard-boiled eggs. Accent with stuffed animals such as chickens, roosters, and pigs.

Suggest a dress code of farm attire for the event (do you have overalls that you've just been aching to wear?).

And, of course, play CDs of country or bluegrass music during meal preparation and dinnertime to complete the mood!

Recipes

MRS. TWEEDY'S HOMEMADE CHICKEN PIE

- 1 frozen pie crust, thawed
- ½ cup onion, chopped
- ½ cup mushrooms, chopped
- 1 cup frozen peas
- 1 cup frozen chopped carrots
- 3 tablespoons butter
- ⅓ cup flour
- ½ teaspoon salt
- ½ teaspoon dried thyme
- ¼ teaspoon pepper
- 2 cups chicken broth
- ¾ cup milk
- Meat from 2 medium deli-roasted chickens

Boil peas and carrots until tender, then drain. In a saucepan, melt butter over medium heat; add onions and mushrooms and cook until tender. Stir in flour, salt, thyme, and pepper. Add chicken broth and milk, and cook until thickened and bubbly, stirring. Add peas and carrots and chicken, and cook until bubbly.

Pour into a 2-quart rectangular baking dish. Place thawed pastry crust over the casserole, and crimp the edges. (If necessary, roll out the pie crust with a rolling pin to make it fit the size of your casserole.) Make several slits for steam. Bake in a 450 degree oven for 15 minutes. Serves 6.

DIRT AND WORMS

- two 4-serving size packages instant chocolate pudding mix
- 2 cups milk
- 1½ cups whipped topping
- one 20-ounce package chocolate sandwich cookies, crushed
- gummy worms

Add milk to a large glass bowl, and whisk in pudding mix. Beat for 2 minutes, until thick. Stir in whipped topping. Spread into a 9x13-inch dish. Cover with crushed cookies. Stick gummy worms into "dirt," and chill until ready to serve. Serves 8-10.

Make Ahead

CHIVE MASHERS

- 1½ pounds russet potatoes
- ¼ cup low-fat sour cream
- 3 tablespoons fresh chives, snipped
- salt and pepper

Peel and quarter potatoes. Cook, covered in a small amount of boiling water for 20 to 25 minutes or until tender. Mash with a potato masher. Add sour cream, chives, salt, and pepper, and mix. Place in microwave-safe casserole dish and refrigerate until reheating to serve. Serves 6.

COOKING TOGETHER

1. Before your guests arrive, remove Chive Mashers from refrigerator.

2. When everyone arrives, remind kids of the importance of washing hands before preparing a meal.

3. Have a few adult volunteers prepare Mrs. Tweedy's Homemade Chicken Pie according to the recipe on page 14. This recipe will take longer than the others, so it's important to begin right away.

4. Enlist a couple of adults to help kids create Dirt and Worms according to the recipe on page 14.

5. When the potpie is placed in the oven, reheat Chive Mashers in the microwave so that it's heated through when the potpies are done.

6. Have the remaining guests set the table and prepare beverages.

7. When everything is ready, move the food to your serving table, and ask someone to pray over your meal. (Don't forget to serve Dirt and Worms for dessert!)

8. After dinner, ask one or two volunteers to make Puffy Pellets (microwave popcorn) and place in bowls in the TV room.

9. While the Puffy Pellets are popping, enlist remaining guests to help with a quick cleanup.

> **Meal Time TalkStarters**
>
> • Which are you more likely to do: try something new (and maybe risky!) or stick with what you know?
> • Do you think "the grass is always greener on the other side of the fence"? Why or why not?
> • Are you more of a lone-ranger chicken or part of a coop? Explain.

LET'S WATCH A MOVIE!

THE PRE-SHOW

Have everyone gather in the area where you'll show the movie. If you've just finished eating dinner, you may want to provide a quick break for people to use the restroom.

When everyone is together, offer beverages and Puffy Pellets to anyone who's ready for a snack. Provide paper bowls or cups as snack containers.

Have adults team up with kids in groups of three to five, and give each group a piece of paper and pen. Ask groups to answer these trivia questions about chickens. Then read the answers aloud so all can compare their answers to the correct ones.

WHEN CHICKENS FLY TRIVIA QUIZ

1. What's a group of chickens called: a flock, a peck, or a peep?
2. Can chicken feathers explode?
3. What is the fleshy piece of hanging skin under a chicken's beak called?
4. Can chickens fly?
5. Once a hen lays an egg, how much time passes before she begins producing another one?

Answers
1. A peep.
2. Yes—this actually happened on a farm in England when a tornado swept chickens up from their coop. (The normal pressure inside the quills was a lot higher than the low air pressure of the tornado.)
3. A wattle.
4. No. Modern chickens have been bred to have more meat in the breast portion, making flying difficult.
5. About 30 minutes.

THE SHOW
Chicken Run

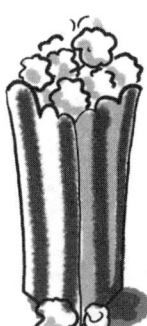

Genre: Adventure/Comedy

Length: 84 Minutes

Rating: G

Plot: Ginger, a clever hen on the Tweedy's chicken farm, is always trying (without success) to mastermind an escape for the chickens on the farm. You see, if a hen doesn't produce enough eggs to satisfy Mrs. Tweedy, she orders that it be killed, a fate Ginger wants to avoid for all of them.

One day, just as things are beginning to look especially grim, circus-star Rocky Rooster accidentally "flies" into the farmyard. Ginger has a brainstorm and makes him promise to help the chickens escape by teaching *them* to fly. There are only two problems: One, Rocky can't really fly—he only appears to when he's shot from a cannon as part of his circus act, and two, chickens can't fly—period.

Time is critical as Mrs. Tweedy, angry about the money they're losing on eggs, decides to start a chicken-pie business instead. Ginger needs to think fast. If Rocky can't keep his promise, how will the chickens escape before they're covered in pie crust?

THE POST-SHOW

After the movie, use some or all of these questions to discuss the spiritual themes in *Chicken Run*.

 Who was your favorite character in this movie, and why?

 Ginger wanted to be free, even before she was in danger of being made into a pie. Why do you think freedom is so important?

 When Rocky told the rats that he could lay eggs, he rationalized to Ginger by saying that he didn't lie—he just left out the truth. Do you agree with his thinking? Why or why not?

 Rocky pretended he could fly so everyone would like him. Have you ever told someone you could do something when you knew you really couldn't? If so, what happened?

Bible Passages
You may want to use these Bible passages during your movie discussion:

- *Exodus 20:16—Tell the truth.*
- *Philippians 2:3-5—Sacrifice for others.*
- *Mark 10:43-45—Serve one another.*

 Tell about a time it would've been easier for you to leave out the truth rather than be completely honest with someone.

 Ginger could have saved herself, but she tried to save every chicken even though it was risky. What do you think you'd have done in her situation? What can we learn from Ginger?

 When Fowler gave Rocky a medal for saving Ginger from the chicken-pie machine, it boosted Rocky's confidence. Tell about someone who's boosted your confidence by something he or she said to you or did for you.

 Rocky was asked to sacrifice his freedom in order to save all of the chickens. How is that like or unlike what Jesus did for us?

PRAYER

End your time together in prayer. Thank God for blessing you with a night together, and pray that God would help you to sacrifice your own wants and needs in order to help others. Have each person pray for someone else in the group; for example, everyone could pray for the person to the right.

Easy Option Meal

If your group isn't inclined to cook, you can still have a "jolly holiday" with another yummy selection: Let your guests build their own roast beef sandwiches by providing deli meat, rolls, cheese, lettuce, tomatoes, and condiments. Complete the meal with chips and a fruit or green salad.

SUPPLIES

Before your Dinner and a Movie event, you may want to talk to everyone who plans to attend and divide up the ingredients list. Keep in mind that some items, such as the steak, cost a lot more than others. Perhaps two people would like to share the cost of the meat, while others each bring a couple of items.

What you'll need: **Names:**

1 jar lemon curd

Poppins' Popovers (serves 8-10)

2 eggs

1 cup milk

1 tablespoon butter

1 cup flour

¼ teaspoon salt

Devonshire Cream (serves 8)

one 3-ounce package cream cheese

1 tablespoon sugar

1 cup heavy cream

pinch salt

Extras

sugar cubes

cream for tea

hot tea (Earl Grey is a popular English variety)

salad greens and sliced salad vegetables

dressing for the salad

lemonade

London Broil (recipe on page 21)

Uncle Albert's Cranberry Scones (recipe on page 22)

Permission to photocopy this page from *Group's Dinner and a Movie: G-Rated* granted for local church use. Copyright © Group Publishing, Inc., P.O. Box 481, Loveland, CO 80539. www.group.com

Recipes

POPPINS' POPOVERS

2 eggs	1 cup white flour
1 cup milk	¼ teaspoon salt
1 tablespoon butter, melted	

Have younger kids identify and select measuring cups and spoons used in this recipe while older kids measure the ingredients. Then assign each child a specific job, such as adding a certain ingredient to the batter, stirring, or spooning the batter into the muffin cups.

Have your young helpers put all ingredients in a large bowl and mix thoroughly without overbeating. Ask a volunteer to fill buttered muffin pans or custard cups halfway. Have an older child put them in a cold oven as you set the heat for 450 degrees. Bake for 15 minutes. (Be sure to have your oven light illuminated. Kids will enjoy watching the popovers raise through the oven door!) Then reduce heat to 350 degrees and bake for another 15-20 minutes. Test one to be sure it's done by removing it from the pan: It should be crisp outside and moist and tender inside. Serves 8-10.

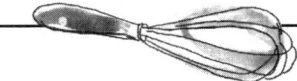

DEVONSHIRE CREAM

one 3-ounce package cream cheese	1 pinch salt
1 tablespoon sugar	1 cup heavy cream

In medium bowl, cream together cream cheese, sugar and salt. Beat in cream until stiff peaks form. Chill. Serve Devonshire Cream and lemon curd with scones. Serves 8.

LONDON BROIL (SLOW COOKER RECIPE)

2 pounds flank steak	1 can condensed tomato soup
1 can condensed cream of mushroom soup	1 package onion soup mix

Place steak in the bottom of a slow cooker, slicing meat if necessary to make it fit. In a medium bowl, mix together mushroom and tomato soups. Pour mixture over beef. Sprinkle onion soup mix over top. Cover and cook on low for 8 to 10 hours. Slice into thin diagonal servings. Serves 6 to 8.

Set the Stage

Turn your gathering area into a Victorian English parlor! Set out teapots filled with colorful real or artificial flowers. Don't own a teapot? Consider what Mary Poppins would do: Days before the party, take your kids on a fun scavenger hunt, searching thrift shops, garage sales, or dollar stores for the perfect teapot treasure.

Add some whimsy to your party by hanging colorful umbrellas upside down from the ceiling and setting others around the room. Guests will enjoy contributing to the mood, so invite them to bring theirs as well.

For artistic fun as guests are arriving, provide colorful sidewalk chalk for kids to decorate your sidewalk and entryway with silly, imaginative pictures.

Set out a basket with these party favors: For each guest, place a peppermint candy in the bowl of a plastic spoon, wrap that end with clear plastic wrap, and secure it with a ribbon and a Scripture note that reads: "A cheerful heart is good medicine" (Proverbs 17:22a).

And, of course, use the Mary Poppins soundtrack as background music while you cook.

Make Ahead

UNCLE ALBERT'S CRANBERRY SCONES

2 cups all-purpose flour
⅓ cup sugar plus extra for sprinkling
1 teaspoon baking powder
¼ teaspoon baking soda
½ teaspoon salt

8 tablespoons unsalted butter, frozen
½ cup dried cranberries
½ cup sour cream
1 large egg

Adjust oven rack to lower-middle position, and preheat oven to 400 degrees. Combine the flour, sugar, baking powder, baking soda, and salt in a large bowl.

Grate the butter into the flour mixture using the large slots of a box grater, then use your fingers to work the butter into the flour mixture—the mixture should resemble coarse meal at this point. Add the dried cranberries.

In a small bowl, whisk sour cream and egg until smooth. Add this mixture to the dry ingredients, and mix until large dough clumps form. Press the dough against the inside of the bowl until it adheres together. (The dough will be sticky in places, and there may not seem to be enough liquid at first—don't worry. Keep pressing.)

Place dough on a lightly floured surface, and pat it into a 7- or 8-inch circle about ¾-inch thick. Sprinkle with sugar. Use a sharp knife to cut into 8 triangles, then place these on a cookie sheet (preferably lined with parchment paper), about 1 inch apart.

Bake until golden, about 15 to 17 minutes. Cool for 5 minutes, and serve warm or at room temperature. Makes 8.

COOKING TOGETHER

1. When guests have arrived, remind kids of the importance of washing their hands before preparing a meal. Then have an adult supervise and assist children in making Poppins' Popovers according to the recipe on page 21.

2. Have a volunteer mix the Devonshire Cream according to the recipe on page 21.

Friendship, Faith, and Fun for All Ages

3. Have a couple of volunteers create a green salad by tossing the lettuce with sliced and chopped vegetables.

4. As the popovers finish baking, remove the London Broil from the slow cooker. Have someone prepare it for the table by slicing it diagonally into thin strips.

5. Ask anyone who isn't cooking to set the table and prepare beverages for everyone.

6. Bring the salad and dressing to the table along with the meat and popovers. Gather everyone around the table, and ask a volunteer to pray over the meal.

7. Ask someone to brew the tea and set out cream and sugar cubes. Serve tea and Uncle Albert's Cranberry Scones with Devonshire Cream and lemon curd during the movie. See recipes on pages 21 and 22.

Meal Time TalkStarters

• Tell about a favorite nanny or baby sitter you had as a child. What made that person special to you?

• Have you ever laughed so hard you just couldn't stop? What was so funny?

• If you could jump into a painting or a drawing and be a part of it, what would it be a picture of? Where would you find yourself?

• Have you ever been to your parent's workplace, or have you ever asked your parent to describe a day at work? What did you learn about your parent after that experience?

LET'S WATCH A MOVIE!

MARY POPPINS

THE PRE-SHOW

Have everyone gather in the area where you'll show the movie. If you've just finished eating dinner together, you may want to provide a quick break for people to use the restroom.

When everyone is together, serve hot tea. Ask a child to assist you in serving cream and sugar cubes while another child offers the scones. Be sure to provide napkins.

Have adults team up with kids in groups of three to five, and give each group a piece of paper and pen. Ask groups to answer these trivia questions relating to Mary Poppins. Then read the answers aloud so all can compare their answers to the correct ones.

MARY POPPINS TRIVIA QUIZ

1. What's the difference between American carousels and European carousels?

2. What does the phrase "catch the brass ring" refer to?

3. How old were the chimney sweeps in England during the 1800s?

4. When and where was the first kite invented?

5. What's the highest number of kites flown on a single line?

6. If you put one penny in the bank on the first day of the month and doubled it every day after that (two pennies the second day, four pennies the next), how much money would you have saved in a 30-day month?

Answers

1. American carousels turn counterclockwise while in England they turn clockwise.
2. In France, riders of early carousels tried to spear gold rings with lances while the carousel rotated at full speed. Later, people would reach out to grab a brass ring as the carousel turned.
3. It was more a matter of size than age. Because chimney openings were so small, some children as young as 4 years old were trained to climb into them to clean them.
4. The first kite was invented about 3,000 years ago in China.
5. A Japanese kite maker flew 11,284 kites on a single line.
6. Over 5 million dollars.

THE SHOW
Mary Poppins

Genre: Family

Length: 139 minutes

Rating: G

Plot: In an Oscar-winning performance, Julie Andrews stars as Mary Poppins, a nanny who is "practically perfect in every way"—that is, according to her good friend Bert and the two mischievous children under her care. But the children's father, a no-nonsense banker with little patience, isn't so sure.

When the wind deposits Mary Poppins on the Banks' doorstep, the adventures begin! She takes the children, Jane and Michael, on outings where unbelievable things happen and lessons are subtly learned. The children delight in every day spent with Mary, but things go awry one day when young Michael decides to spend his two-pence to feed the birds rather than invest it in the bank where his father works. Mr. Banks loses his job as a result. Will Mary Poppins be able to save the day? Watch to find out!

THE POST-SHOW

After the movie, use some or all of these questions to discuss the spiritual themes in *Mary Poppins*.

 Who did you like best in this movie, and why? Which character do you think you're the most like, and why?

 Which adventure would you have liked to go on with Mary or Bert? Explain why.

What effect did Mr. Banks' personality have on the rest of his family? What effect did his family have on him?

 What did Mary Poppins mean when she said that a spoonful of sugar helps the medicine go down? Can you think of an example where that's true in your life?

 When talking to them about their father, Bert tells the children that cages come in all sizes, some of them "bank sizes." What do you think he meant by that? What are things that can make you feel "caged in"?

 Mr. Banks thought that losing his job was the very worst thing that could happen, but it turned out to be a very good thing. Why? When has a difficult circumstance turned out to be a positive experience in your life?

 Michael and Jane learned that they needed to trust their father. How can we learn to trust God, our heavenly father?

 Imagine that you wrote a story called "Mary Poppins: Part 2." Where would the wind have taken Mary this time?

Bible Passages
You may want to use these Bible passages during your movie discussion:

- *Ephesians 6:2—Honor your parents.*
- *Isaiah 55:2—Don't waste time and money on things that don't satisfy you spiritually.*
- *Matthew 6:19-21—Invest in things that have eternal value.*
- *1 John 2:15-16—Don't love the things of this world.*

PRAYER

End the evening by praying together. Ask for prayer requests. Encourage each person to share one specific way to put into practice the lessons learned from the movie *Mary Poppins*. Have each person pray for someone else in the group; for example, everyone could pray for the person to the right.

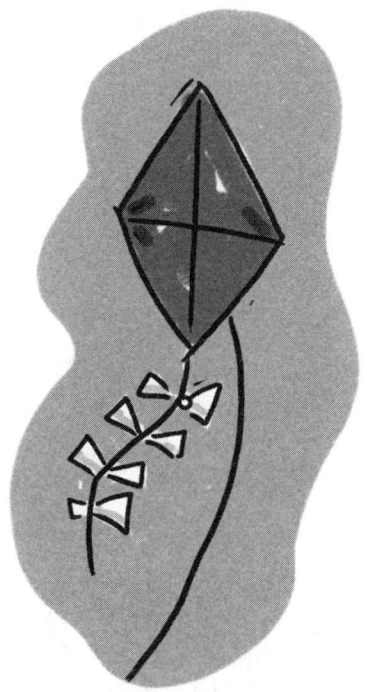

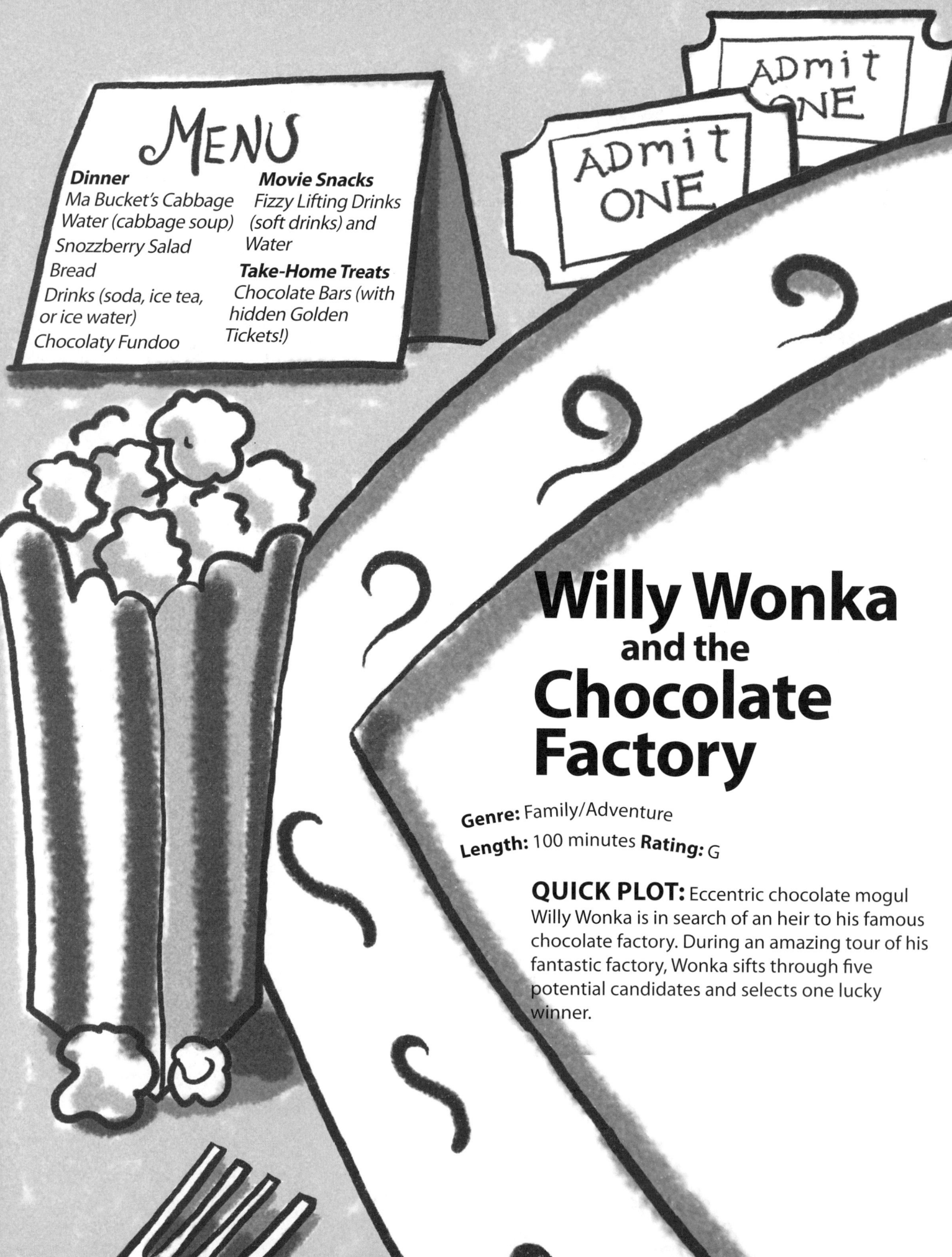

MENU

Dinner
Ma Bucket's Cabbage Water (cabbage soup)
Snozzberry Salad
Bread
Drinks (soda, ice tea, or ice water)
Chocolaty Fundoo

Movie Snacks
Fizzy Lifting Drinks (soft drinks) and Water

Take-Home Treats
Chocolate Bars (with hidden Golden Tickets!)

Willy Wonka and the Chocolate Factory

Genre: Family/Adventure
Length: 100 minutes **Rating:** G

QUICK PLOT: Eccentric chocolate mogul Willy Wonka is in search of an heir to his famous chocolate factory. During an amazing tour of his fantastic factory, Wonka sifts through five potential candidates and selects one lucky winner.

SUPPLIES

Before your Dinner and a Movie event, you may want to talk to everyone who plans to attend and divide up the ingredients list. Keep in mind that some items may cost a lot more than others. Perhaps two people would like to share the cost of those ingredients, while others each bring a couple of items.

What you'll need:	Names:
Snozzberry Salad (serves 8)	
1 bag of frozen mixed berries	_____
1 container of whipped topping	_____
½ cup chopped walnuts	_____
2 bananas	_____
Chocolaty Fundoo (serves 10)	
fondue pot	_____
wooden skewers	_____
butter	_____
one 12-ounce package semisweet chocolate chips	_____
½ cup heavy whipping cream	_____
1 container fresh strawberries	_____
3 apples	_____
1 bag pretzel sticks	_____
1 angel food cake	_____
loaf of bread	_____
butter	_____
Ma Bucket's Cabbage Water (recipe on page 28)	_____
Hidden Golden Ticket (recipe on page 29)	_____

Easy Option Meal

If your group would prefer not to cook, pick up a quick rotisserie chicken dinner at your local grocery store. Add coleslaw and mashed potatoes from the deli, choose a loaf of bread, and the meal is complete!

 Permission to photocopy this page from *Group's Dinner and a Movie: G-Rated* granted for local church use. Copyright © Group Publishing, Inc., P.O. Box 481, Loveland, CO 80539. www.group.com

Friendship, Faith, and Fun for All Ages

Set the Stage

With a theme like chocolate and candy…it's easy to have fun! Toss handfuls of candy kisses on tables, fill jars with brightly colored candies, and use twinkle lights to create a fun atmosphere. Vibrant candy colors are key for this movie's motif!

Before guests arrive, wrap heavy-duty paper plates as if they were gigantic candies, using different colors of cellophane or bright, clear gift wrap. Use curling ribbons on each side. Scatter these randomly throughout the rooms you'll be using, or hang them from the walls and ceiling. Accent with lots of colorful balloons hanging from the ceiling and lying on the floor.

Make a large "lollipop" by inserting a stick into a round plastic-foam ball then covering the ball with colored plastic wrap. Tie a ribbon around the neck of the stick. Create several of these to arrange in tall jars.

For an especially memorable event, dress up like Willy Wonka or another character in the movie and encourage your guests to do the same. Kids will have a blast as Oompa Loompas—use face paint to color their faces orange, and tint their hair green with colored hair spray.

SNOZZBERRY SALAD

1 bag frozen mixed berries, partially thawed

1 container whipped topping

2 bananas, sliced

½ cup chopped walnuts

Pour the berries into a large bowl, and gently fold in the whipped topping, as much as desired. Add sliced bananas and the walnuts to the berry mixture. Stir gently until mixed. Serves 8.

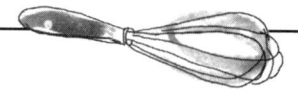

CHOCOLATY FUNDOO

one 12-ounce package semisweet chocolate chips

2 tablespoons butter

½ cup heavy whipping cream

Melt chocolate in a double broiler. Stir in butter and whipping cream until smooth. Transfer the chocolate mixture to a fondue pot, or keep on the stove over low heat until ready to serve. Guests will use wooden skewers to pierce and dip sliced bananas, apples, strawberries, pretzels, and angel food cake in chocolate mixture. Serves 10.

MA BUCKET'S CABBAGE WATER (CABBAGE SOUP)

3 tablespoons olive oil

½ onion, chopped

2 cloves garlic, chopped

2 quarts water

4 teaspoons chicken bouillon

1 teaspoon salt, or to taste

½ teaspoon black pepper, or to taste

½ head cabbage, cored and coarsely chopped

one 14.5-ounce can Italian-style stewed tomatoes, drained and diced

one 15-ounce can red kidney beans, drained

In a large stockpot, heat olive oil over medium heat. Stir in onion and garlic; cook until onion is transparent, about 5 minutes. Stir in water, bouillon, salt, and pepper. Bring to boil, and then stir in cabbage. Simmer until cabbage wilts, about 10 minutes. Stir in tomatoes and beans. Return to boil, and then simmer 15 to 30 minutes, stirring often. Serves 8.

HIDDEN GOLDEN TICKET

chocolate bars (one for each guest) | yellow slips of paper
tape

Carefully unwrap chocolate bars, preserving the wrappers. Using yellow slips of paper, create "golden tickets" with an affirming message on each one. For example, you might write "It was fun spending time with you during our dinner and a movie!" Wrap a ticket around each chocolate bar, carefully re-wrapping the bar so that the ticket doesn't show, then seal the wrapper with a small piece of clear tape.

COOKING TOGETHER

1. Just before guests arrive, begin melting chocolate chips in a double-boiler. Be careful not to allow any water to get into the chocolate, or it will harden. Also, if the soup was prepared well ahead of time and refrigerated, now's the time to reheat it.

2. When all the guests have arrived, remind kids of the importance of washing their hands before preparing a meal.

3. Enlist three or four kids to help an adult prepare the Chocolaty Fundoo according to the recipe on page 28. Kids can slice bananas and cut angel food cake into small chunks using butter knives, and they can arrange the dipping pieces on a couple of plates or trays.

4. Have an adult and child work together to make the Snozzberry Salad according to the recipe on page 28.

5. Have a volunteer prepare the bread by slicing it and spreading butter on each slice. Wrap the bread in foil and put it in the oven at 350 degrees. Bake it until the butter is melted—about 10 minutes.

Meal Time TalkStarters

- *Imagine that you're a candy inventor. What would your best candy creation taste like? What would it look like? What would you call it?*
- *Talk about a favorite childhood memory associated with a sweet treat.*
- *What would it be like if the only food on earth was candy? Explain.*
- *Tell about a time you won a special prize.*

6. Have others set the table with soup bowls and small plates and prepare the dinner beverages.

7. Invite everyone to gather at the table. Ask a volunteer to pray over the meal—then enjoy dinner together!

8. After dinner, have volunteers help clear bowls away and then bring the fundoo to the table, along with wooden skewers and trays of food for dipping.

LET'S WATCH A MOVIE!

THE PRE-SHOW

Have everyone gather in the area where you'll show the movie. If you've just finished eating dinner together, you may want to provide a quick break for people to use the restroom.

When everyone is together, serve Fizzy Lifting Drinks for refreshment during the movie.

Have adults team up with kids in groups of three to five, and give each group a piece of paper and pen. Ask groups to answer these trivia questions about candy. Then read the answers aloud so all can compare their answers to the correct ones.

CANDY TRIVIA QUIZ

1. What candy flavor do most Americans prefer?

2. Cotton candy, originally called fairy floss, is made with only one ingredient. What is it?

3. Which two holidays account for the most candy sales?

4. The first lollipop machines could make 40 lollipops per minute. How many can today's machines make?

5. About how many candy canes are sold around Christmastime?

6. What is the most popular color of gummi candy?

Answers
1. Chocolate (berry and vanilla tied for second).
2. Sugar.
3. Halloween and Easter.
4. Almost 6,000 lollipops per minute.
5. 2 billion—enough to circle the world, end to end, more than 4½ times!
6. Red.

THE SHOW
Willy Wonka and the Chocolate Factory

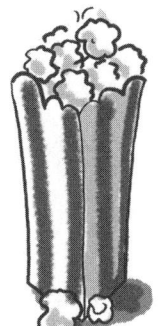

Genre: Family/Adventure

Length: 100 minutes

Rating: G (Very young children may be uneasy about a spooky boat scene.)

Plot: Kind-hearted Charlie Bucket lives with his impoverished mother and grandparents. Charlie's mom provides for the family through cleaning laundry. When not in school, Charlie also helps bring food to the table, tobacco to his favorite family member, Grandpa Joe, and he even earns an occasional chocolate Wonka Bar through his paper route.

The reclusive candy mogul, Willy Wonka, has locked down his factory from all outsiders to protect his secrets from his rival, Mr. Slugworth. After a number of years, Wonka announces to the world that five lucky children who find a golden ticket inside the wrapper of a Wonka Bar will be allowed to tour his factory. A widespread panic ensues, and people rush to buy Wonka Bars and find a winning ticket.

Can you believe it? Charlie finds the last of the five tickets! Charlie and Grandpa Joe join four other children and their parents on a fanciful tour of Wonka's factory. Expecting to simply have a good time, Charlie gets much more than he ever hoped for during this trip of excitement and adventure.

THE POST-SHOW

After the movie, use some or all of these questions to discuss the spiritual themes in *Willy Wonka and the Chocolate Factory*.

 What's your favorite scene from the movie? Were there any parts you didn't like?

 How was the craze over Wonka Bars similar to or different from crazes over today's toys or game systems?

Bible Passages
You may want to use these Bible passages during your movie discussion:
- Romans 5:5—Our hope in Christ can't disappoint us.
- Romans 15:13—Hope, joy, and peace come from trusting God.
- 1 Timothy 6:17—Put hope in God, not earthly wealth.
- Luke 12:15—Don't be greedy.

 What makes certain things become popular? What makes people want those things?

 When have you wanted something so much that you acted unreasonably in your attempt to get it? What would have been a better way to handle that?

 Tell about a time you had too much of a good thing. What lesson did you learn from that experience?

 Why do you think Charlie was chosen to inherit the candy factory? Do you think he deserved it? Why or why not? Do you think we usually get what we deserve in life? Explain your answer.

 Mr. Slugworth was able to tempt most of the children. What tempts you to do the wrong thing? How do you handle that temptation?

 What are you hoping for in life? What is your "Golden Ticket"?

 As a Christian, what can you hope for that only God can offer?

PRAYER

End the evening by praying together. Ask for prayer requests. Encourage each person to share one specific way to put into practice the lessons learned from the movie *Willy Wonka and the Chocolate Factory*. Have each person pray for someone else in the group; for example, everyone could pray for the person to the right.

Before your guests leave, have one of the children give a chocolate bar to each guest. They'll be pleased and surprised when they discover their "winning" tickets!

SUPPLIES

Before your Dinner and a Movie event, you may want to talk to everyone who plans to attend and divide up the ingredients list. Keep in mind that some items, such as the pork chops, may cost a lot more than others. Perhaps two people would like to share the cost of the meat, while others each bring a couple of items.

Easy Option Meal

Though authentic schnitzels take only about a half an hour to cook, this classic movie is three hours long—so you might opt for a quicker meal. Put together an Austrian-style dinner without even turning on your oven by purchasing ready-cooked rotisserie chickens, German potato salad, and a cabbage or cucumber salad from the grocery deli. Buy fresh rye bread and an herbed spread to accent the meal, and serve apple turnovers from the bakery.

What you'll need:	Names:
Maria's Favorite Schnitzel With Noodles (The first four ingredients need to be prepared ahead of time. Serves 8)	
8 boneless pork sirloin chops or chicken breasts	
dry white bread crumbs (about 1 cup)	
4 eggs	
flour (about 1 cup)	
oil for frying	
2 lemons	
16 ounces egg noodles	
butter	
sprig of fresh parsley	
salt	
plastic bags	
Do-Re-Mi Drinks (makes 3 quarts)	
apple juice (2 quarts)	
mineral seltzer water (1 quart)	
Flibbertijibbets Snack Mix (makes 4 cups)	
1 cup each of assorted dried fruits, nuts, dry cereal, and chocolate chips	
1 loaf bakery rye bread, sliced	
Extras coffee and tea	
(Make Ahead) I-Have-Confidence Cucumber Salad (recipe on page 36)	
(Make Ahead) Odl-Lay-Hee-Hoo Apple Strudel (recipe on page 36)	
(Make Ahead) Salzburg Spread (recipe on page 37)	

Permission to photocopy this page from *Group's Dinner and a Movie: G-Rated* granted for local church use. Copyright © Group Publishing, Inc., P.O. Box 481, Loveland, CO 80539. www.group.com

Friendship, Faith, and Fun for Small Groups

MARIA'S FAVORITE SCHNITZEL WITH NOODLES

- 8 boneless pork sirloin chops or chicken breasts
- 1 cup dry white bread crumbs, finely crumbled
- 4 eggs
- oil for frying
- flour (about 1 cup)
- 2 lemons
- 16 ounces egg noodles
- butter
- fresh parsley
- salt
- plastic bags

Place one boneless pork chop or half a chicken breast in a plastic zippered bag, but do not seal. Place bag on a hard solid surface like a countertop or cutting board. Pound the first piece of meat in the bag with a meat mallet or the side of a rolling pin until it is very thin. Repeat with the other 7 pieces of meat.

Coat meat in flour, then dip floured meat in small bowl of whisked eggs.

Coat the moistened meat with bread crumbs.

Heat enough cooking oil in a large frying pan so schnitzels will "float" in the oil while cooking. Using metal tongs, transfer the meat to the pan, turning meat while browning. Keep the oil hot, and cook until the schnitzels are golden brown and cooked through—about 3-5 minutes. Transfer cooked schnitzels to a tray covered with paper towels to drain for a minute and then to a warmed platter for serving.

Boil water, and cook egg noodles according to package directions. Drain and add butter, salt, and chopped or torn fresh parsley.

Serve schnitzel and noodles with lemon wedges. Serves 8.

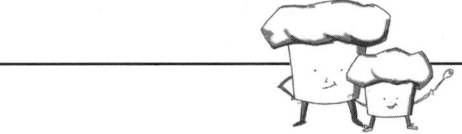

DO-RE-MI DRINKS

- apple juice (2 quarts)
- mineral seltzer water (1 quart)

In a pitcher, mix two parts apple juice with one part mineral seltzer water. Makes 3 quarts.

FLIBBERTIJIBBETS SNACK MIX

- 1 cup assorted dried nuts, such as almonds, walnuts, sunflower kernels, and macadamias
- 1 cup assorted dried fruits, such as raisins, pineapple chunks, and chopped dates
- 1 cup dry cereal
- 1 cup chocolate chips

Measure all ingredients into a large serving bowl, and mix or toss lightly with a wooden spoon. Makes 8 half-cup servings.

Set the Stage

Make "the hills come alive" at your Austrian-themed dinner and a movie! Check out Austrian travel and picture books from your local library, and place these on tables in your gathering area. Borrow CDs of Austrian folk music or Viennese Strauss waltzes for background music—or surprise your guests with music from the original Von Trapp Family Singers, which is available on CDs online. The Sound of Music soundtrack would also be appropriate, of course!

Austrians very rarely use paper plates, so plan to use real dishes and glasses instead. Decorate with flowers and more flowers! Austrians adore flowers, and no city or country dinner party would be complete without fresh bouquets throughout the rooms.

Provide paper, markers, and a picture of the Austrian flag for kids to copy as they create miniature flags to place about the room as guests arrive.

During dinner, kids and adults will enjoy practicing the German terms for "please" (bitte—bit-teh) and "thank you" (danke—dahn-keh). At the end of the evening, bid your guests farewell with "auf wiedersehen" (awf-vee-der-zehn).

In Austrian homes, guests remove their shoes at the door and the host provides them with slippers to wear for the evening. Put a fun twist in this custom by purchasing fun, comfy socks for guests to wear during the dinner and movie and to take home as mementos of their Austrian tour!

I-HAVE-CONFIDENCE CUCUMBER SALAD

4 large cucumbers	1 teaspoon salt
4 tablespoons cider vinegar	½ teaspoon pepper
2 tablespoons sugar	1 cup sour cream

Peel cucumbers, and cut them into very thin slices. Place cucumber slices in a medium-sized bowl. In a small bowl, mix the vinegar, sugar, salt, and pepper. Pour the liquid over the cucumbers, stir, and allow it to marinate for about 20 minutes. Stir again, and then drain off the extra liquid. Mix in the sour cream and serve. Serves 8.

(Note: This recipe tastes best made an hour or less before serving to keep the cucumbers crisp.)

ODL-LAY-HEE-HOO APPLE STRUDEL

4-6 medium-sized tart apples (granny smith or other firm apple)	¼ cup finely chopped pecans or walnuts
1 package frozen puff pastry dough (2 large squares)	¼ cup raisins
¼ cup sugar	½ cup butter, melted
1 tablespoon fresh lemon juice	2 tablespoons fine unflavored dry bread crumbs
1 teaspoon cinnamon	confectioner's sugar
1 tablespoon flour	

Preheat oven to 375 degrees, and lightly grease a large baking sheet. Allow pastry dough to thaw according to package directions while preparing the strudel filling.

Peel, core, and thinly slice apples to make about 4 cups. In a large bowl combine apples with lemon juice, sugar, cinnamon, flour, nuts, and raisins.

To assemble strudel, place one square of pastry dough on waxed paper and unfold. Brush the ⅓ of dough closest to you with melted butter, and sprinkle with 1 tablespoon of the bread crumbs. Place half of the apple mixture on top of bread crumbs, and brush the rest of dough with melted butter. Begin rolling the dough over the apples and continuing rolling up until you make a "log." Pinch and tuck in edges as needed to seal, then carefully place on greased baking pan. Repeat these steps to assemble your second strudel.

Brush the strudels with melted butter, and bake in the oven for 40 minutes or until golden brown. Brush again with melted butter halfway through cooking

time and after removing from oven. Cool, and dust tops of strudels with confectioner's sugar before serving. Serves 6-8.

SALZBURG SPREAD

- 8 ounces cream cheese
- 6 tablespoons butter, softened
- 3 tablespoons sour cream
- 1½ teaspoons paprika
- 1 small onion finely chopped
- 2 tablespoons dill or sweet gherkins, finely chopped
- 1 tablespoon capers, finely chopped
- ½ teaspoon prepared mustard
- salt and pepper to taste

Finely chop onion and gherkins. Place butter in mixing bowl and mix for 1-2 minutes until it's soft and fluffy. Add the cream cheese, sour cream, paprika, mustard, salt, and pepper, and gently mix until blended. Stir in the chopped onion, gherkins, and capers. Cover and let sit for a few hours in the refrigerator before serving.

This is a common spread in Austria and is served in local restaurants with fresh rye or pumpernickel bread or rolls. Makes about 1 cup.

COOKING  TOGETHER

1. An hour or two before your guests arrive, prepare meat for schnitzel according to the recipe on page 35. Follow steps to coat the meat with flour and bread crumbs, then refrigerate breaded meat until time to cook.

2. When everyone arrives, remind guests of the importance of washing their hands before preparing a meal. Invite a couple of kids along with an adult volunteer to prepare a pitcher of the Do-Re-Mi Drinks according to the recipe on page 35. Refrigerate the finished drink to serve during the movie.

3. Have a few kids create the Flibbertijibbets Snack Mix according to the recipe on page 35. Encourage them to be creative as they combine their own unique, tasty mixture! Set the finished mix aside to serve during the movie.

4. Remove the breaded meat from the refrigerator, and heat enough cooking oil in the large frying pan so the schnitzels can "float" in the oil while cooking. When the oil is hot, have a couple of volunteers team up to fry the meat according to the recipe on page 35.

5. Have a volunteer boil water and cook the egg noodles according to package directions. Drain and add butter, salt, and parsley.

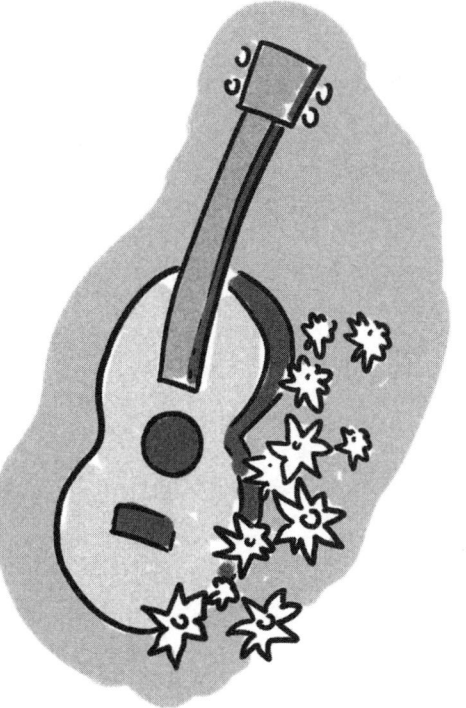

Meal Time TalkStarters

- In The Sound of Music, Maria sings about her favorite things. What are your favorite things? favorite places to visit? favorite songs? favorite foods?
- The von Trapp family had seven children. What do you think is better, to have a family with lots of brothers and sisters, or just a few, or to be an only child. Explain your answer.
- Share a dream that you have achieved. Share a dream you have yet to achieve.
- Where is your favorite place to go to be alone with God?

6. As schnitzels and noodles are being cooked, ask kids to set the table with the I-Have-Confidence Cucumber Salad, Rye Bread With Salzburg Spread, bowls of fresh lemon wedges, and beverages.

7. Have everyone gather at the table, and ask someone to pray over the meal. Before starting, encourage guests to try their schnitzel the traditional Austrian way with fresh lemon juice drizzled on top—then enjoy!

8. After the meal, enlist cleanup help from your guests so you can all play a game and watch the movie. Let everyone know you'll be serving Odl-Lay-Hee-Hoo Apple Strudel during the movie's scheduled intermission (mmm… can't wait!).

THE PRE-SHOW

Have everyone gather in the area where you'll show the movie. If you've just finished eating dinner together, you may want to provide a quick break for people to use the restroom.

When everyone is together, serve Flibbertijibbets Snack Mix and Do-Re-Mi Drinks to anyone who's ready for a snack.

Have adults team up with kids in groups of three to five, and give each group a piece of paper and pen. Ask groups to answer these trivia questions related to *The Sound of Music*. Then read the answers aloud so all can compare their answers to the correct ones.

THE SOUND OF MUSIC TRIVIA AND ACTIVITY QUIZ

1. What is the name of the musical scale the song "Do-Re-Mi" teaches?

2. Austria is a German-speaking country. What does the German word "strudel" mean?

3. True or false: The real Maria von Trapp appears in the movie *The Sound of Music*.

4. What famous composer was born in Salzburg, Austria?

5. *The Sound of Music* is based on the experiences of the real von Trapp family. In what U.S. state did the real family eventually settle?

6. What was the original purpose of yodeling?

(Any yodelers in your group? See who can perform this yodel from *The Sound of Music*: "Lay ee odl lay ee odl lay hee hoo!")

THE SHOW
The Sound of Music

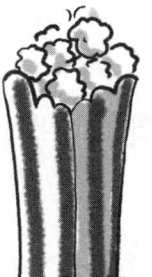

Genre: Musical/Family

Length: 175 minutes

Rating: G (Best suited for children 5 and over due to political themes and extended length of the movie.)

Plot: Julie Andrews stars as Maria, a young Austrian who desperately wants to become a nun. Though she's a dedicated novice, Maria's intense personality and carefree spirit don't quite fit the calm, structured life of the abbey. The Reverend Mother sees Maria's good heart and potential, however, and sends her to be a governess for the seven unruly children of a widowed naval officer. Shocked to find a family governed by laws instead of laughter, a determined Maria teaches the children how to enjoy life by singing and playing—even when times are difficult. But just as the music and joy begin to take root in their hearts, Maria discovers that her own heart is softening for the captain. Confused, she realizes that she must find God's ultimate plan for her life and returns, without saying goodbye, to the abbey.

But this is a love story with a happy ending. Again the Reverend Mother uses wisdom and insight to help Maria see where she really belongs, and Maria returns to the family. She and the captain profess their love to each other and wed, but by that time Hitler has annexed Austria and the captain is called to return to naval service. The von Trapps are faced with a decision: Should they compromise their principles in order to maintain social standing and wealth, or should they sacrifice their worldly goods in order to escape with their integrity intact? Using inventive means and their unique musical talent, the family makes their choice.

THE POST-SHOW

After the movie, use some or all of these questions to discuss the spiritual themes in *The Sound of Music*.

 What was your favorite scene or song from the movie? Why?

 Why do you think Maria became a "problem" at the abbey? Tell about a time you felt like you didn't "fit in." How did others treat you? How did it make you feel?

Answers

1. Solfege is used to connect specific one-syllable sounds with each note on a scale. *Do* is the first note in the scale. *Re* is next. Then *Mi,* and so on.
2. Whirlpool.
3. True. Maria makes a cameo appearance, walking in the square as Julie Andrews sings the song "I Have Confidence."
4. Wolfgang Amadeus Mozart.
5. Vermont, where they built the Trapp Family Lodge (still in operation today) in the mountain area of Stowe.
6. Long ago, it was used to spread news from one mountain to the other in the Austrian and Swiss Alps. Certain sounds had specific meanings.

Why do you think Captain von Trapp was portrayed as a stern disciplinarian in the movie? How could you tell the captain loved his children even though he was strict with them?

 Maria defied the captain's wishes and allowed his children to romp through Salzburg, sing in public, and spend lazy afternoons in the mountains. Do you think it was right or wrong of her to do this? Why?

 Captain von Trapp and Maria escape from Austria with the children. If you knew you would lose your home and everything you had in order to stand up for what you believed in, could you do it?

Bible Passages

You may want to use these Bible passages during your movie discussion:

- Proverbs 16:9—The Lord determines our steps.
- Psalm 37:4—Take delight in the Lord.
- Psalm 13:6—Sing to the Lord.
- Jeremiah 29:11—The Lord has plans for us.

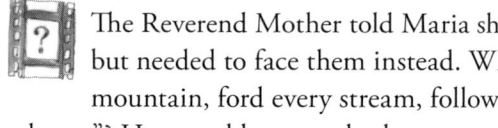 The Reverend Mother told Maria she couldn't hide from her problems but needed to face them instead. What does it mean to "climb every mountain, ford every stream, follow every rainbow, till you find your dream"? How could you apply that same advice to your own life?

 The von Trapps' flight from the Nazis can be compared to Mary and Joseph's flight from King Herod, who wanted to destroy the baby Jesus. What similarities do you think there are between the stories? What do you think it must feel like to become a refugee in another country?

 Why do you think Maria needed to be sent away from her comfort zone in the abbey to the "real world" in order to discover her true purpose? How is this true in our own lives?

PRAYER

End the evening by praying together. In keeping with the musical theme of *The Sound of Music*, ask guests to think of a song everyone is familiar with that you could all sing together in prayer. Common hymns and favorite Christian children's songs would be great choices. Join hands in a circle, and sing your prayer and praises together to the Lord.

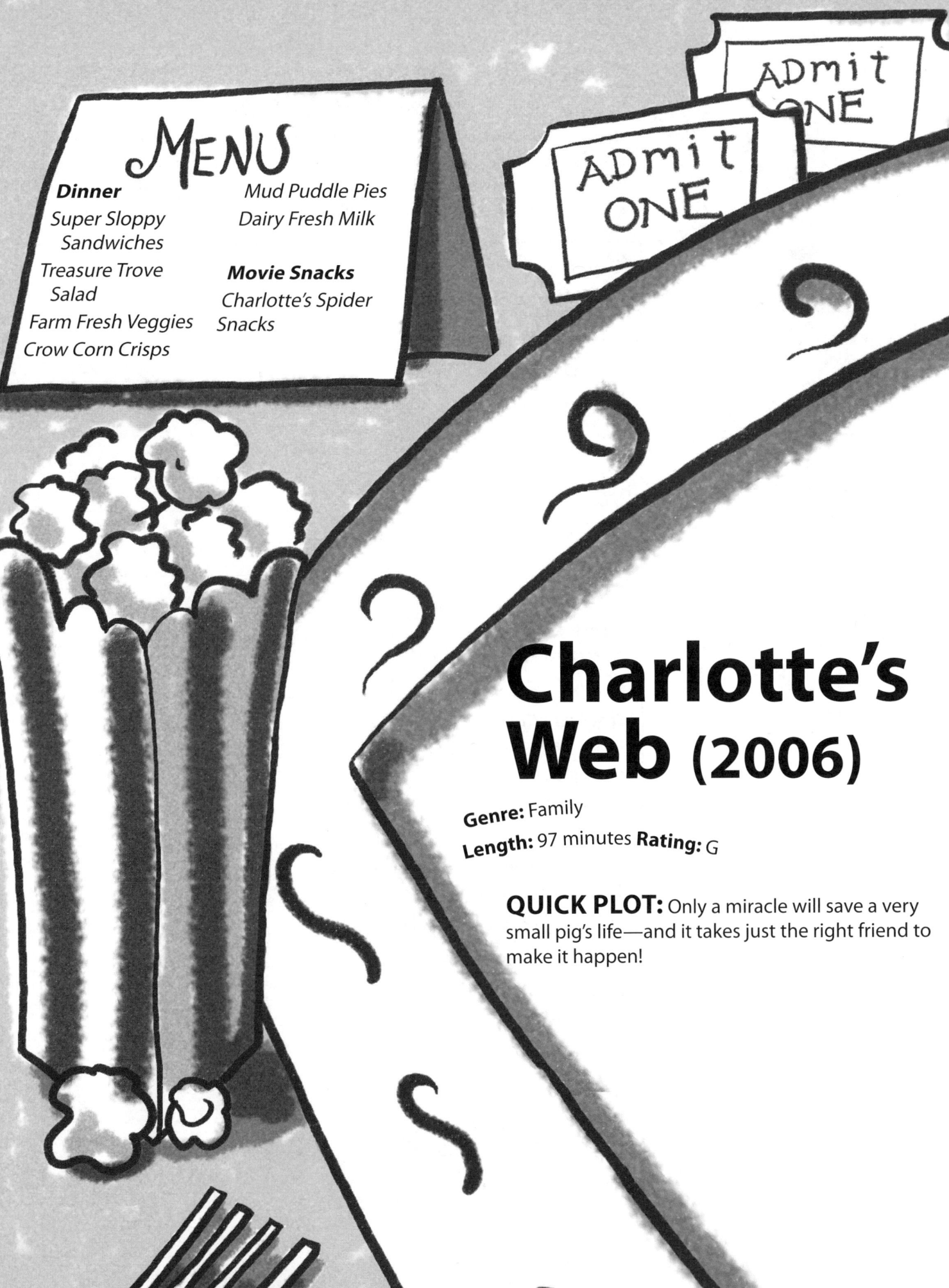

Easy Option Meal

For a kid-friendly dinner without much cooking, pick up three containers of pre-made sloppy Joe meat in the supermarket meat section. Include a fresh veggie tray and a pre-mixed fruit salad from the deli, add corn chips and hamburger rolls, and you have a meal! Just heat up the meat to make the sandwiches, and serve. Complete your barnyard-theme dinner with individual chocolate pudding cups for dessert and pretzel sticks and marshmallows for movie snacks.

SUPPLIES

Before your Dinner and a Movie event, you may want to talk to everyone who plans to attend and divide up the ingredients list. Keep in mind that some items, such as meat, may cost a lot more than others. Perhaps two people would like to share the cost of those ingredients, while others each bring a couple of items.

What you'll need: | **Names:**

Super Sloppy Sandwiches (serves 8)
- 2 pounds ground beef
- 8 hamburger buns
- 1 small onion
- one 15-ounce can tomato sauce
- ½ cup ketchup
- ½ cup barbecue sauce
- 2 tablespoons dry mustard
- 2 tablespoons Worcestershire sauce
- 2 tablespoon white vinegar

Farm Fresh Veggies
- baby carrots
- celery

Crow Corn Crisps
- 1 large bag of corn chips

Dairy Fresh Milk
- ½-1 gallon whole milk
- ½-1 gallon reduced fat milk

Charlotte's Spider Snacks (serves 12)
- 1 bag of large marshmallows
- 1 large bag of thin stick pretzels
- 1 can chocolate frosting

Extras
- soda, water
- paper plates, napkins, cups
- plastic utensils

Make Ahead **Treasure Trove Salad (recipe on page 43)**

Make Ahead **Mud Puddle Pies (recipe on page 44)**

Permission to photocopy this page from *Group's Dinner and a Movie: G-Rated* granted for local church use. Copyright © Group Publishing, Inc., P.O. Box 481, Loveland, CO 80539. www.group.com

Recipes

SUPER SLOPPY SANDWICHES

- 2 pounds ground beef
- 1 small onion, finely chopped
- one 15-ounce can tomato sauce
- ½ cup ketchup
- ½ cup barbecue sauce
- 2 tablespoons dry mustard
- 2 tablespoons Worcestershire sauce
- 2 tablespoons white vinegar
- 8 hamburger buns

Brown meat in large skillet; drain grease. Add next 7 ingredients, and simmer covered over low heat for about 10 to 12 minutes. Stir occasionally.

Serves 8.

CHARLOTTE'S SPIDER SNACKS

- 1 bag of large marshmallows
- 1 large bag of thin stick pretzels
- 1 can chocolate frosting

Create sweet "spiders" by inserting 8 pretzel sticks around a marshmallow to resemble spider legs (the marshmallow is the body). Spoon about a cup of frosting into a plastic sandwich bag, and cut the point from a corner of the bag with scissors. Squeeze frosting through the notched corner to create a spider web design on a serving tray. Serves 12.

Make Ahead

TREASURE TROVE SALAD

- 2 large cans mandarin oranges, drained
- 1 large can crushed pineapple, drained
- 2 cups sweetened coconut flakes
- 2 cups colored miniature marshmallows
- 2 cups sour cream
- 2 cups chopped pecans (optional)

For best flavor, mix up this yummy salad an hour before serving. Drain juice from oranges and pineapple, then place all ingredients in a large bowl and stir. Serves 12.

Set the Stage

It's time to head to the farm! Re-create the feel of Zuckerman's farm in your own home by decorating with a country theme. Purchase or borrow a few hay bales from a nearby farm, or pick up bedding hay at your local pet store and make a haystack just outside your doorway. Assemble a scarecrow using old clothes stuffed with wadded newspapers and supported by a broomstick, and place him along with a few gourds or corncobs at your entrance. Indoors, decorate your table with a red-checkered tablecloth, white paper plates, napkins, and plastic utensils and cups. Accent your gathering rooms with gourds, pumpkins, or any other harvest produce.

Invite your guests to wear jeans or overalls—any farm clothing will do! And, for a special treat, purchase inexpensive bandannas at your local hobby store for guests to wear and take home.

Set the country mood with CDs of country or square-dance music playing in the background.

Make Ahead

MUD PUDDLE PIES

1 large package instant chocolate pudding mix

3 cups milk

2 packages individual graham cracker crusts (12 total)

1 small squeeze bottle caramel ice-cream sauce

Mix chocolate pudding mix and milk in a bowl according to package directions. Spoon pudding into individual crusts, and then squirt a squiggly line of caramel sauce on top. Keep refrigerated until ready to serve. Serves 12.

COOKING TOGETHER

1. As people arrive, remind them of the importance of washing their hands before preparing a meal.

2. Designate one team of three adults to prepare the Super Sloppy Sandwiches according to the recipe on page 43.

3. Set kids up at a small table or counter area with the marshmallows and pretzel sticks, and enlist one adult to help kids make Charlotte's Spider Snacks according to the instructions on page 43. Ask them to make at least one "spider" for each guest.

Have the adult help each child take a turn squeezing the frosting bag to make a round circle of frosting on the tray, starting from the inside and working out toward the edge. (See picture 1.) Make the web design by using the flat side of a dinner knife and pulling lines from the middle to the edge of the tray. (See picture 2.)

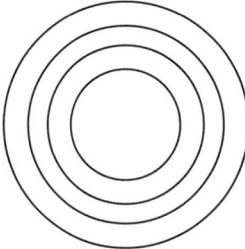

Picture 1

Picture 2

When the web is completed, have the kids arrange the "spiders" on the web to serve during the movie.

4. Have an adult and child pair up to prepare the Farm Fresh Veggies. As the adult cuts the vegetables, have the child arrange them creatively on a plate.

5. Ask a volunteer to set the dining table with place settings and Dairy Fresh Milk.

6. Have a couple of volunteers pour Crow Corn Crisps (corn chips) into a bowl to set out with Treasure Trove Salad and veggies for buffet-style serving.

7. Have two adults assemble Super Sloppy Sandwiches by spooning the saucy meat mixture into hamburger buns and placing them on a large tray. Add this to the buffet table.

8. Dinner is ready! Invite your guests to serve themselves in the buffet line then gather at the table where a volunteer will pray over the meal.

9. Cleanup is easy! Throw paper and plastic products away, and place leftovers in the refrigerator.

10. Serve individual Mud Puddle Pies for dessert before the movie. Set out Charlotte's Spider Snacks and bowls of extra marshmallows and pretzels to enjoy during the movie.

> **Meal Time TalkStarters**
> *• Complete this sentence: "The farm animal that most resembles my personality is a _____ because _____."*
> *• How many words can you think of that mean "wonderful"? Tell about someone you know who could be described with those words.*
> *• Share a time a friend helped you when you were in great need. How did that person prove he or she was a true friend?*

LET'S WATCH A MOVIE!

CHARLOTTE'S WEB

THE PRE-SHOW

Have everyone gather in the area where you'll show the movie. If you've just finished eating dinner together, you may want to provide a quick break for people to use the restroom.

When everyone has gathered, remind them that Charlotte's Spider Snacks and beverages are available for refreshments during the movie. Be sure to provide napkins!

Have adults team up with kids in groups of three to five, and give each group a piece of paper and pen. Ask groups to answer these trivia questions about barnyard animals. Then read the answers aloud so all can compare their answers to the correct ones.

BARNYARD TRIVIA QUIZ

Answers
1. Four.
2. Eight (but even with so many eyes, most spiders have very poor vision).
3. Bucks (females are called does and babies are called pups or kittens).
4. A clutch.
5. Official major league baseballs are made with wool yarn wrapped around a cork center.
6. Six to 7 hours a day.
7. Yes. Horses can lock their legs in position and then relax to sleep.
8. Here are some possibilities: is, so, me, go, gem, pie, peg, mope, poem. What others did you come up with?

1. How many toes does a pig have on each hoof?
2. How many eyes do most spiders have?
3. What are male rats called?
4. What are goose eggs in a nest called?
5. Sheep's wool is used to make what official league sport item?
6. How many hours a day does a cow spend eating?
7. Can horses sleep standing up?
8. Try this word challenge—how many words can you make in one minute using only the letters SOME PIG?

THE SHOW
Charlotte's Web

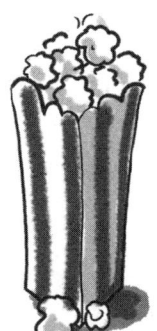

Genre: Family

Length: 97 minutes

Rating: G

Plot: E.B. White's beloved story comes to life in this live-action adaptation. Wilbur is "some pig." Born the runt of the litter, he is rescued from certain death by Fern, a young girl who convinces her father to let her keep him as a pet. She names him Wilbur, and he lives with her until his growing size necessitates his move to Uncle Zuckerman's barnyard. Alone among animals who don't accept his rambunctious ways, he is finally befriended—by a spider.

Charlotte is a wise and wonderful friend who announces Wilbur's value by weaving words about him in her spider web. But Wilbur's days are numbered once again as the Zuckermans make plans for a delicious smoked winter ham, and Charlotte realizes it will take a miracle to save him. She devises a plan to convince the farmer that Wilbur's life is worth sparing—and Wilbur is entered in the county fair.

Do miracles really happen? Charlotte shows Wilbur what it really means to have worth, and even in her short life she's able to demonstrate what loyalty and lasting friendship really mean.

THE POST-SHOW

After the movie, use some or all of these questions to discuss the spiritual themes in *Charlotte's Web*.

 Who was your favorite character in the movie? Why?

Bible Passages

You may want to use these Bible passages during your movie discussion:

- *John 15:13—A friend loves.*
- *John 15:15—Jesus is our friend.*
- *1 Corinthians 12:24-26—Care for one another.*
- *Proverbs 29:23—Humility brings honor.*

 Would you like to have someone like Charlotte or Wilbur as a friend? Why or why not?

 Complete this sentence: "A friend is _____."

 How did Charlotte show that she was a good friend? How do you show others that you're a good friend?

 How does Jesus show us that he's our friend? What can we do to be a good friend to Jesus?

 Charlotte's words convinced the humans to believe Wilbur's life was worth saving. How does God let you know your life is important?

 The Bible says in Proverbs 16:24 (NLT) "Kind words are like honey—sweet to the soul and healthy for the body." What effect did Charlotte's words have on Wilbur? How can we use words that will be sweet and healthy?

 What did Charlotte do for Wilbur that is similar to what Jesus has done for us?

PRAYER

End the evening by praying in a special way together. Hand sticky notes and pens to each person. Make a circle, and have one person stand in the middle. Have each person on the outside of the circle write one encouraging or affirming word on his or her paper and then "stick" that word on the person in the middle. Continue until each person has had a turn in the middle. End your time by joining hands and praying in a circle together, thanking God for the lessons you learned from the movie *Charlotte's Web*.

Friendship, Faith, and Fun for All Ages

SUPPLIES

Before your Dinner and a Movie event, you may want to talk to everyone who plans to attend and divide up the ingredients list. Keep in mind that some items may cost a lot more than others. Perhaps two people would like to share the cost of those items, while others each bring a couple of items.

Easy Option Meal
No time to cook? For an easy and quick meal, pick up some corn chips, a raw veggie party tray, yellow gelatin cups, and a pre-made apple pie at your local supermarket to go with the hot dogs.

What you'll need:	Names:
Toto Dogs	
hot dogs	_____
hot dog buns	_____
Scarecrow's Snack	
fresh or frozen corn on the cob	_____
Rainbow Munchies	
cherry tomatoes	_____
baby carrots	_____
yellow bell peppers	_____
sugar snap peas	_____
purple grapes	_____
ranch dressing (for dipping)	_____
Colorful Colas	
clear soda or flavored water	_____
assorted food coloring	_____
Extras	
ketchup, mustard, relish	_____
butter	_____
wooden skewers	_____
lollipops	_____
Activity items	
two 1-liter empty plastic soda bottles	_____
heavy tape (such as duct tape)	_____
Make Ahead **Yellow Brick Molds (recipe on page 50)**	_____
Make Ahead **There's-No-Place-Like-Home Apple Pie (recipe on page 51)**	_____

Permission to photocopy this page from *Group's Dinner and a Movie: G-Rated* granted for local church use. Copyright © Group Publishing, Inc., P.O. Box 481, Loveland, CO 80539. www.group.com

49

Recipes

Set the Stage

Take your guests "somewhere over the rainbow!" Nothing is black and white there—so go wild with color! Create a vibrant dining room with paper plates, cups, tablecloths, and utensils in a wide variety of colors. Use streamers and balloons, and sprinkle red glitter or confetti (think ruby slippers) on the dining room table to immerse your guests in a rainbow of colors.

Enlist your kids to prepare the entryway for guests by drawing yellow bricks with sidewalk chalk, or use yellow construction paper taped to the sidewalk to make a yellow brick road to your door.

Post a homemade sign at the beginning of the walk that says "Now leaving Kansas," another along the walk that says "Follow the yellow brick road," and one at the door that says "Welcome to Somewhere Over the Rainbow."

RAINBOW MUNCHIES

cherry tomatoes	sugar snap peas
baby carrots	purple grapes
yellow bell peppers	ranch dressing

Wash all vegetables and fruits. Cut peppers into strips. Arrange on a tray in a colorful arch, like a rainbow, or create your own vibrant design! Place dressing in a small container to serve with the munchies.

COLORFUL COLAS

| clear soda or flavored water | assorted food coloring |

Pour soda into glass or clear plastic cup. Add one or two drops of food coloring and stir (it doesn't take much to create a vibrant tint!).

YELLOW BRICK MOLDS

| two 8-ounce packages of lemon or pineapple powdered gelatin | water |
| | plastic ice-cube trays |

Kids will love to help create a yellow brick road that's actually edible! If possible, let your kids assist you with this make-ahead menu item.

Make gelatin according to package instructions for Jigglers (the result is a firmer set). Pour gelatin into plastic ice-cube trays, filling halfway. Let cool in refrigerator for at least 3 hours. To unmold, place ice-cube tray in shallow warm water for 5-10 seconds to loosen, then invert cubes ("bricks") onto tray and arrange as a miniature brick road. Bricks can also be made by pouring gelatin into two 13x9 pans and cutting into block shapes after setting. Makes about 80 bricks.

Make Ahead

THERE'S-NO-PLACE-LIKE-HOME APPLE PIE

1 single crust for 9-inch pie	1 egg
Filling:	1 cup sour cream
3 cups of apples, peeled and chopped	1 teaspoon vanilla extract
	Crumb Topping:
2 tablespoons flour	⅓ cup sugar
¼ teaspoon salt	⅓ cup flour
¾ cup white sugar	1 teaspoon cinnamon
¼ teaspoon ground nutmeg	2 tablespoons butter

Preheat oven to 400 degrees. Core, peel, and chop apples. Place prepared pie crust in 9-inch pie plate. Combine egg, sour cream, and vanilla in a bowl. In another bowl stir together flour, salt, sugar, and nutmeg. Add egg mixture to dry ingredients, and mix well. Stir in chopped apples, and then spoon into unbaked pie crust. Bake at 400 degrees for 15 minutes then reduce to 350 degrees for 30 more minutes.

Prepare crumb topping while pie is cooking: Measure sugar, flour, cinnamon, and butter in a bowl, and combine using a pastry blender until crumbly.

Remove pie from oven, and increase temperature to 400 degrees. Sprinkle crumb topping over pie, and return to oven for 8-10 minutes. Cool on rack, then refrigerate. Serve either warm or chilled. Serves 8.

COOKING  TOGETHER

1. Before your group arrives, prepare the grill and set out all utensils and ingredients needed for preparing the meal.

2. As guests arrive, remind them of the importance of washing their hands before handling food, and invite any child volunteers to strip the leaves and silky threads from the corn into a trash bag. Have them break each ear in half to prepare for cooking.

3. Designate one adult to grill the Toto Dogs (or prepare in the kitchen using a preferred method for hot dogs).

4. Have an adult cut the peppers into slices while children arrange the veggies and fruit on a tray in a rainbow pattern as suggested in the recipe on page 50. Place the ranch dressing in a bowl next to the Rainbow Munchies for easy dipping.

Meal Time TalkStarters

- *Are you more likely to explore the other side of the rainbow, or do you believe there's no place like home? Tell us why.*
- *Tell us about a wonderful dream you've had that seemed real.*
- *Are you more like a lion who needs courage, a scarecrow who needs a brain, a tin man who needs a heart, or a person who needs to find the way? Explain.*
- *What's the difference between a wish and a prayer?*

5. Have an adult volunteer release the "yellow bricks" from their molds, and ask kids to arrange the bricks on a tray according to instructions on page 50.

6. Ask another adult to cook corn on the cob for four to five minutes in boiling salted water, timing preparation so the corn is done just as dinner is served. To make Scarecrow's Snack, place a wooden skewer into the bottom of each cooked corn cob—you now have corn on a stick for easier handling! Be sure to have lots of butter and salt available for guests to put on the finishing touches.

7. Encourage kids and adults to experiment with color as they prepare their own Colorful Colas as described on page 50. Remember—it takes only a drop or two to make a fun color!

8. Have remaining guests prepare a buffet-style serving area. Remember to include buns and condiments for the Toto Dogs.

9. Ask a volunteer to pray over the meal, then let guests serve themselves and move to the dining table.

10. Cleanup is a snap. Place leftovers in the refrigerator, and toss paper plates in the trash.

11. You may opt to serve There's-No-Place-Like-Home Apple Pie now, but your guests will probably enjoy it more after the movie during your discussion time.

LET'S WATCH A MOVIE!
THE WIZARD OF OZ

THE PRE-SHOW

Have everyone gather in the area where you'll show the movie. If you have just finished eating dinner together, you may want to provide a quick break for people to use the restroom.

When everyone is together, offer lollipops and additional drinks to anyone who's ready for snacks.

Then, for a fun activity before the movie, make a tornado! Have a couple of adult volunteers fill an empty plastic soda bottle about ¾ full. Have them invert another empty plastic bottle over the opening of the filled bottle, ensuring the spouts are lined up. Provide duct tape to securely fasten the bottles together in this position.

Have a child volunteer turn the bottles upside down so the bottle with the water is on top. Show the child how to swirl the bottles in a circular motion (not up and down) really fast. The water in the bottles will move in the same way that air moves in a tornado. Pass the bottles around the room so others can try making a tornado in a bottle, then follow up with these trivia questions:

TORNADO TRIVIA QUIZ

1. What is this movement of water called?

2. How fast can the winds of a tornado travel?

3. How fast can a tornado move on the ground?

4. True or False: A tornado can "suck up" fish and frogs from ponds and later "rain" them back to earth.

5. What state has the most number of tornados per area?

a. Kansas

b. Texas

c. Florida

Answers

1. A whirlpool.
2. Up to about 300 miles per hour.
3. An average of 35 miles per hour (as fast as people drive on many city roads), but up to 70 miles per hour (about as fast as people drive on the highway).
4. True! People have been showered with fish and frogs (and even tomatoes and corn!) when clouds carrying them from tornados finally release them, miles later, in a rainstorm.
5. Florida (Texas ranks first in overall number of tornadoes).

THE SHOW
The Wizard of Oz

Genre: Family/Musical

Length: 101 minutes

Rating: G (Tornado scene and scenes with the wicked witch and wizard may be too frightening for children under 8.)

Plot: Dorothy, a restless girl who lives on a farm in Kansas, feels that she's misunderstood by the adults in her life. She's about to run away from home when a tornado hits, picking up her house with her in it and dropping it in the middle of a fantastic place called Oz. Luckily for Dorothy, her faithful dog Toto is by her side throughout this adventure—and she makes lovable, whimsical friends along the way.

But this land on the other side of the rainbow isn't as carefree as she imagined it would be—Dorothy is pursued by a wicked witch, and her dream becomes a nightmare as she tries desperately to get back home.

Bible Passages
You may want to use these Bible passages during your movie discussion:

- *Psalm 31:24—God gives courage.*
- *Psalm 48:14—God is our guide.*
- *James 1:12—God rewards perseverance.*
- *Psalm 37:4—God gives us the desires of our hearts.*

Her journey takes her and her new friends along a yellow brick road to Emerald City, home of a self-proclaimed wizard. In spite of the hopes they've pinned on this mere man, the wizard can't help Dorothy return to Kansas, and she discovers that she had the ability to solve her own troubles all along. But her journey through Oz isn't fruitless, for Dorothy has learned lessons about love, courage, thoughtfulness, and loyalty—and she brings those lessons home with her when she finally wakes from her fantastic dream.

THE POST-SHOW

After the movie, use some or all of these questions to discuss the spiritual themes in *The Wizard of Oz*. Serve There's-No-Place-Like-Home Apple Pie for dessert during your discussion.

 What was your favorite scene in the movie? your favorite character? favorite song? Why?

 If you were suddenly dropped in a strange land with only three possessions in your basket, what would you want them to be? Why would you choose those items?

 Dorothy had friends to help her during her journey. Explain how your friends help you in the adventures of your life—the fun and the difficult ones.

 How does having Jesus as your best friend help you on your journey in life?

 At the beginning of the movie, Dorothy wanted to discover life "over the rainbow." Why did she want to leave home? What do you think she was looking for?

 Tell about a time you felt like running away from home. What were you looking for that you didn't have? How does God help us find our way back home?

 By the end of the movie, Dorothy decided that "there's no place like home." Do you agree with her? Why do you think she changed her mind?

 Dorothy put faith in the wizard to help her get back home, but he never had the power to help her in the first place. In what people or things do we sometimes misplace our faith? As Christians, where does our faith belong?

Why do you think the wicked witch was so cranky? Is it ever OK to be so cranky to others? Explain.

PRAYER

End the evening by praying together. Stand in a circle and link arms like Dorothy and her friends did as they skipped through the forest. Encourage each person to think of one thing he or she would ask God for to help on the road of life he or she is on right now. Take turns praying a one-sentence prayer such as "Lord, I need courage" or "Lord, I need wisdom." Close by thanking God for giving you guidance and strength for all of the journeys ahead!

SUPPLIES

Before your Dinner and a Movie event, you may want to talk to everyone who plans to attend and divide up the ingredients list. Keep in mind that some items may cost a lot more than others. Perhaps two people would like to share the cost of those ingredients, while others each bring a couple of items.

What you'll need:	Names:
Checkered Flagwiches (serves 8)	
8 slices of wheat bread	_____
8 slices of white bread	_____
8 ounces cream cheese	_____
¾ pound deli-sliced ham	_____
1 cucumber, sliced	_____
Lightning Lemonade (makes 2 liters)	
½ cup sugar	_____
3 cups pineapple juice	_____
½ cup lemon juice	_____
1 liter ginger ale	_____
Tow Mater's Tractor Tippin' Taters (serves 8)	
1 package frozen tater tots or waffle fries	_____
½ of a 1.25-ounce chili seasoning packet	_____
ketchup	_____
Kachow Dip and Chips (serves 12)	
pita chips (at least a handful per person)	_____
2 pounds processed cheese (such as Velveeta), cut up	_____
8 ounces cream cheese, cut up	_____
one 4-ounce can green chiles	_____
1 envelope taco seasoning mix	_____
16 ounces chunky salsa	_____
Flo's Soda	
12 ounces (1 can) root beer per person	_____
1-2 scoops chocolate ice cream per person	_____
Make Ahead **Race Car Cake (recipe on page 59)**	_____

Easy Option Meal

For an easy racetrack meal, pick up a submarine sandwich for each person, or order one extra-long sub sandwich that'll feed everyone. Flo's Soda is a quick, easy drink (chocolate root beer floats), and Kachow Dip can be as simple as spicy salsa from a jar. Store-bought cookies and soda will complete the meal—so let the race begin!

 Permission to photocopy this page from *Group's Dinner and a Movie: G-Rated* granted for local church use. Copyright © Group Publishing, Inc., P.O. Box 481, Loveland, CO 80539. www.group.com

Friendship, Faith, and Fun for Small Groups

TIP:
You can use any meat or toppings you'd like for creative Checkered Flagwiches—just don't make them too thick or they won't stay together.

CHECKERED FLAGWICHES

8 slices of wheat bread	¾ pound deli-sliced ham
8 slices of white bread	1 cucumber, sliced
8 ounces cream cheese	

Cut the crusts off the bread. Spread cream cheese on the bottom piece of bread, and then top with ham and cucumbers. Cover with a piece of bread of the opposite color. Cut each sandwich into 9 or 12 squares (depending on how big your slices of bread are). Rearrange the squares of the sandwiches by flipping over some of the squares so they resemble a checkered flag, alternating white and wheat. Serves 8.

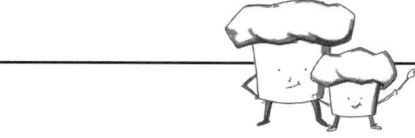

TOW MATER'S TRACTOR TIPPIN' TATERS

1 package frozen tater tots or waffle fries	ketchup
½ of a 1.25-ounce chili seasoning packet	

Cook tater tots or fries according to package directions. Once cooked, sprinkle with the seasoning. Serve with ketchup. Serves 8.

LIGHTNING LEMONADE

½ cup sugar	½ cup lemon juice
¼ cup water	1 liter ginger ale
3 cups pineapple juice	

In a saucepan, heat the water over medium heat, and stir in the sugar, stirring until the sugar dissolves. Combine with the pineapple and lemon juice. Just before serving, slowly add ginger ale, and mix in a large pitcher. Makes 2 liters.

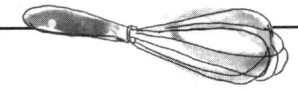

KACHOW DIP AND CHIPS

2 pounds processed cheese (such as Velveeta), cut up

8 ounces cream cheese, cut up

one 4-ounce can green chiles

1 envelope taco seasoning mix

16 ounces chunky salsa

pita chips (enough for expected number of guests)

Combine the first five ingredients in a slow cooker and turn to low heat, stirring occasionally. Serve with chips. Serves 12.

FLO'S SODA

12 ounces (1 can) root beer per person

1-2 scoops chocolate ice cream per person

Serve these chocolate root beer floats for a fun movie drink. Simply place a scoop or two of chocolate ice cream in each glass and slowly pour root beer on top. Add a straw or a long spoon.

Make Ahead

RACE CAR CAKE

2 loaves of pound cake

2 tubs vanilla frosting

food coloring

4 chocolate sandwich cookies

black or red licorice strips

chocolate-coated candies

Remove cakes from pans. Cut 3 inches off of the end of one loaf (this piece will not be used). Diagonally cut 2 inches off of the top of one end of this loaf. Set this cake on top of the whole loaf, to look like a car. Spread vanilla frosting over the "windows" of the car—the front diagonal windshield, the back window,

and the side windows. Use the licorice to line the edges of these windows. Add food coloring to the remaining frosting—whatever color car you'd like! Cover the rest of the car with the colored frosting.

Stick 4 chocolate sandwich cookies on the sides of the car for wheels. Use the chocolate-coated candies for head and tail lights. Use the licorice strips to create racing stripes and even create a number on the hood of the car. Serves 12.

Set the Stage

Decorate Nascar style! Create pennants with construction paper, and write the names of the cars from the movie on them. Hang black-and-white checkered flags on the walls—you can create them by weaving black and white construction paper together and attaching them to dowels. If kids are your decorators, they could have a lot of fun with both of these as craft projects.

Greet your guests with a homemade "Radiator Springs" highway sign on your front door, and label the dining area with a large banner that says "The Pit Stop." If you have any toy cars or classic car paraphernalia, such as posters, place these around your meeting area. If you have a DVD with footage from a car race, have this playing on your TV as guests arrive.

COOKING TOGETHER

1. Before your guests arrive, assemble and frost the Race Car Cake according to directions on page 59.

2. Once guests arrive, remind them of the importance of washing their hands before preparing a meal.

3. Have an adult and a child team up to prepare Tow Mater's Tractor Tippin' Taters according to the recipe on page 58. You'll want to get these in the oven right away in order to serve with the meal.

4. Enlist an adult to help kids make the Checkered Flagwiches according to the recipe on page 58. Be sure the adult does all the cutting while kids spread the cream cheese and place sandwich ingredients on the bread. Have the kids arrange the squares into checkered patterns on serving plates.

5. Have an adult and a couple of kids team up to make Lightning Lemonade according to the recipe on page 58.

6. Have one or two more guests assemble the Kachow Dip according to the recipe on page 59. Be sure the slow cooker is set on low so the dip is ready for a movie snack after dinner.

7. Have any remaining guests set the table with dinnerware and beverages.

8. When dinner is ready, have someone say a prayer over the meal and dig in!

9. After dinner, ask a couple of guests to prepare Flo's Soda for movie snack-time according to the recipe on page 59.

10. Have the remaining guests pitch in to clear the table for a speedy cleanup!

Meal Time TalkStarters

- Describe your absolute dream car. Why is it your favorite?
- Tell about a road trip you'll never forget. Was it fun? Did you get stranded somewhere? Who went with you?
- Have you ever visited a place that you didn't want to leave? Where was it?
- If you could win an award for any one thing, what would you want that award to be? Why?
- Which do you prefer, life in the fast lane or a Sunday drive down a quiet country road? Why?

LET'S WATCH A MOVIE!

THE PRE-SHOW

Have everyone gather in the area where you'll show the movie. If you've just finished eating dinner together, you may want to provide a quick break for people to use the restroom.

When everyone is together, serve Kachow Dip and Chips and Flo's Soda to anyone who's ready for a snack. Be sure to provide napkins.

Have adults team up with kids in groups of three to five, and give each group a piece of paper and pen. Ask groups to answer these trivia questions about transportation. Then read the answers aloud so all can compare their answers to the correct ones.

TRANSPORTATION TRIVIA QUIZ

1. How much does the world's most expensive car cost?

2. Which of the following has actually been clocked as the fastest piece of motorized furniture?

a. a motorized armchair boat

b. a wheeled sofa with a motor

c. a rocket-powered lawn chair

3. What is the fastest anyone has ever ridden a motorcycle—while blindfolded? (Don't try this!)

4. What year was Ford's Model T first available to purchase?

5. In which states does Route 66 begin and end? (For extra credit: What are all the states it goes through?)

Answers
1. $10 million—the asking price for a 1930 Bugatti Type 41 Royale Kellner Coach!
2. b. A motorized sofa in England has been clocked at 87 mph—and it's even licensed to travel on public roads!
3. 164.87 mph! A record set by Billy Baxter in 2003 in Wiltshire, England.
4. 1908.
5. It begins in Illinois and ends in California—going through Missouri, Kansas, Oklahoma, Texas, New Mexico, and Arizona on the way.

THE SHOW
Cars

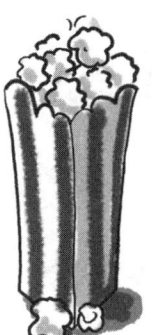

Genre: Family

Length: 116 minutes

Rating: G

Plot: Rookie hotshot race car Lightning McQueen is at the top of his game—he's tied in a race with the top two race cars around, and he's on his way to the tiebreaker showdown. Being a celebrity, Lightning travels in style, cruising down Route 66 in the comfort of a custom trailer. But when he accidentally becomes separated from the trailer, he unintentionally tears up the asphalt of a forgotten little town called Radiator Springs.

The sheriff of the town catches Lightning in this act of destruction, and Lightning is sentenced to community service. But this hot rod doesn't have time for that—he's desperate to get back to his fast-paced life where he can prove himself on the racetrack and accumulate more trophies. He resents his punishment, and the slow-paced, simple life of the town's inhabitants just worsens his attitude. But after spending time with the cars of the town and making deep friendships, Lightning begins to realize that the things he's been chasing—awards, money, and fame—aren't the most important things in life.

Bible Passages
You may want to use these Bible passages during your movie discussion:

- *Psalm 18:27—Be humble.*
- *Proverbs 27:2—Don't praise yourself.*
- *Matthew 7:2—Don't judge others.*
- *Mark 10:31—The last will be first.*
- *1 Timothy 6:6-8—Be content.*

THE POST-SHOW

After the movie, use some or all of these questions to discuss the spiritual themes in *Cars*.

 Which character in this movie reminds you of yourself? In what way?

 Which character would you most like to be friends with? Why?

 Lightning makes judgments about Mator and other rusty cars based on what they look like on the outside. Some of them also made judgments about Lightning. What did they learn once they got to know each other?

 Is it right or wrong to judge people from their appearances? Explain your answer.

 Lightning loves moving fast. Has anyone ever suggested you should slow down a little? What do you think about a suggestion like that?

What does Lightning find in Radiator Springs that he hasn't found in other areas of his life? How does it make him feel?

 Getting praise from others made Lightning happy. Do you think he could be happy by praising others instead? Why or why not? In what ways can you praise or encourage the people you know?

 Lightning finds peace in Radiator Springs, but not everyone can live in a sleepy out-of-the-way town. How can you find peace where you are *right now?*

PRAYER

End the evening by praying together. Ask for prayer requests. Encourage each person to share one specific way to live out a lesson learned from *Cars*. Have each person pray for someone else in the group; for example, everyone could pray for the person to the left.

SUPPLIES

Before your Dinner and a Movie event, you may want to talk to everyone who plans to attend and divide up the ingredients list. Keep in mind that some items may cost a lot more than others. Perhaps two people would like to share the cost of those ingredients, while others each bring a couple of items.

What you'll need: **Names:**

Trees and Vines (serves 8-10)
- 2 pounds spinach pasta, such as fettuccini or spaghetti
- 2 pounds broccoli
- 2 tablespoons olive oil
- ¼ cup butter
- 3 cloves garlic
- 1 cup fresh Parmesan or Romano cheese
- ¼ cup fresh basil leaves, torn

Jungle Juice
an assortment of juices, such as:
- pineapple juice
- apple juice
- mango juice
- guava juice
- orange juice

Banana Canoe Sundaes
- 1 banana per person
- 1 carton vanilla ice cream
- 1 small jar maraschino cherries
- 1 package chocolate-covered pretzel sticks
- 1 can chocolate syrup

Jungle Critter Crunch (makes 8 cups)
- 1 cup animal crackers
- 1 cup bear-shaped graham crackers
- 4 cups air-popped popcorn (made ahead of time)
- 1 cup dried cherries
- 1 cup chocolate coated candies

Shipwrecked Pineapple (recipe on page 67)
 Make Ahead

Easy Option Meal

If you'd rather not work hard as the Robinsons for your dinner, pick up a tropical island feast from a local grocery-store deli instead. Include a tropical fruit salad, a side salad such as coleslaw, Asian chicken wings, and coconut macaroons. We still recommend the Banana Canoe Sundaes—they're that easy!

Permission to photocopy this page from *Group's Dinner and a Movie: G-Rated* granted for local church use. Copyright © Group Publishing, Inc., P.O. Box 481, Loveland, CO 80539. www.group.com

TREES AND VINES
(PASTA AND BROCCOLI)

2 pounds spinach pasta, such as fettuccini or spaghetti

2 pounds broccoli

2 tablespoons olive oil

¼ cup butter

3 cloves garlic, minced

1 cup fresh Parmesan or Romano cheese

¼ cup fresh basil leaves, torn

salt and pepper

Prepare pasta according to package directions, and set aside. Wash broccoli, and cut it into small "trees." Put broccoli in a covered casserole, add several tablespoons of water, and microwave for 5 minutes. In a large pan, melt oil and butter. Add garlic and cook for 1 minute. Add noodles, broccoli, basil, and cheese to the pan and mix. Season with salt and pepper to taste. Serves 8-10.

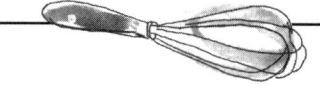

BANANA CANOE SUNDAES

1 banana per person

vanilla ice cream

maraschino cherries

chocolate-covered pretzel sticks

chocolate syrup

Have each person create his or her own canoe sundae. Slice a banana in half lengthwise, and arrange slices side by side in a bowl to create a "canoe." Place several small scoops of ice cream into the middle of the canoe. Stick several chocolate-covered pretzel sticks into the ice cream for paddles. Top with cherries and chocolate syrup as desired.

JUNGLE CRITTER CRUNCH

1 cup animal crackers

1 cup bear-shaped graham crackers

4 cups popcorn

1 cup dried cherries

1 cup chocolate coated candies

Mix all ingredients in a large bowl for a movie snack. Have fun with the ingredients—see what different animal snacks you can find, such as animal-shaped fruit snacks, to add to the mix! Makes 8 cups.

Permission to photocopy this page from *Group's Dinner and a Movie: G-Rated* granted for local church use.
Copyright © Group Publishing, Inc., P.O. Box 481, Loveland, CO 80539. www.group.com

Friendship, Faith, and Fun for Small Groups

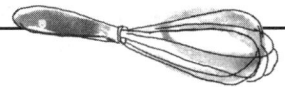

JUNGLE JUICE

an assortment of juices, such as:	mango juice
pineapple juice	guava juice
apple juice	orange juice

Allow each guest to create his or her own version of Jungle Juice by mixing a number of different tropical juices. Have fun with it—have a contest for the tastiest drink and the most creative drink name!

SHIPWRECKED PINEAPPLE

| 1 whole pineapple | 4 kiwis |
| 12 strawberries | |

Slice the pineapple directly in half. Scoop the pineapple out of the shell, cutting into chunks. Slice the strawberries into quarters, and slice the kiwis into bite-sized pieces. Toss the pineapple, strawberries, and kiwis together, and place into the hollowed pineapple. Seal in plastic wrap and chill until ready to serve. Serves 8.

Set the Stage

The setting of Swiss Family Robinson is a beach, a tropical jungle, and an elaborate treehouse. You can create an island feel by using lots of bamboo, raffia, and tropical colors.

For example, line your entryway with tiki torches. Hang raffia skirts (available at most party goods stores) from doorframes or wrap them around your serving table. Use tissue paper to make brightly colored paper flowers.

Create an indoor jungle by twisting brown crepe paper tightly to look like vines, stringing them between walls or from the ceiling, and stapling construction-paper leaves to the twisted paper. Cut palm tree silhouettes from butcher paper to tape to your walls, and arrange as many green leafy plants as you can around the area where you'll watch the movie.

The Robinsons' island is filled with exotic animals, so set out stuffed animals such as zebras, parrots, or even snakes to keep your guests company! Have a CD with jungle sound effects playing in the background during meal preparation and dinner.

COOKING TOGETHER

1. Just before guests arrive, pop some popcorn for the Jungle Critter Crunch.

2. When guests have arrived, remind everyone of the importance of washing their hands before handling food.

3. Assign several volunteers to make the Trees and Vines according to the recipe on page 66. Have them cook the pasta right away so it'll be ready when the other food is. While one person boils the pasta, the others can chop and cook the broccoli and gather the other ingredients.

GROUP'S DINNER AND A MOVIE: G-RATED

Meal Time TalkStarters

• If you were stranded anywhere in the world, where would you want to be? Why there? Who would you want with you?

• Not many of us have been shipwrecked, but we all experience close calls. Tell about one time you came close to, or survived, a disaster.

• Imagine you're about to move to a new country and you can only take one suitcase with you. What would be in that suitcase?

• What's one great adventure you'd like to have in your life?

4. Have one adult help kids create the Jungle Critter Crunch according to the recipe on page 66. Be sure to make a large bowl available, as well as the popcorn you've popped ahead of time.

5. Ask an adult volunteer to set up your Jungle Juice "staging area" by arranging your array of juices (suggested in the supply list on page 67) and cups.

6. Have another adult volunteer set out ingredients for Banana Canoe Sundaes to be ready for dessert. (Don't set out the ice cream yet!)

7. Have remaining guests set the table, including the Shipwrecked Pineapple.

8. When all of the food is ready, allow each guest to create his or her own Jungle Juice mix from ingredients provided—encourage everyone to be creative and invent his or her own new tropical drink!

9. When everything is ready, move the food to your serving table, and ask someone to pray over your meal.

10. After eating, make cleanup easy by asking all to pitch in.

11. Set out ice cream, and invite your guests to build their own Banana Canoe Sundaes to enjoy either at the table or during the trivia game and movie.

LET'S WATCH A MOVIE!

THE PRE-SHOW

Have everyone gather in the area where you'll show the movie. If you've just finished eating dinner together, you may want to provide a quick break for people to use the restroom.

When everyone has gathered, have Jungle Critter Crunch and beverages available to anyone who wants snacks during the movie. Be sure to provide fun napkins along with paper cups to hold the Critter Crunch.

Have adults team up with kids in groups of three to five, and give each group a piece of paper and pen. Ask groups to answer these trivia questions about shipwrecks, islands, and castaways. Then read the answers aloud so all can compare their answers to the correct ones.

SHIPWRECKS, ISLANDS, AND CASTAWAYS TRIVIA QUIZ

1. Who did the author of *Swiss Family Robinson* name the Robinson family after?

2. What single shipwreck had over 1,600 survivors?

3. Imagine you're walking along the beach and you find a brand-new bicycle that had somehow washed ashore in a crate. The same day, you learn that a shipwreck had occurred miles off the coast—and the ship had been carrying merchandise including bicycles. Since the ship is sunk anyway, can you keep the bike?

4. True or false: The story of the Swiss Family Robinson has a sequel (a part 2).

5. Which country has the most large islands?

6. Name three movies, TV shows, or books that have to do with shipwrecks or castaways.

Answers

1. Robinson Crusoe.
2. 1,660 were saved from Italian ocean liner *Andrea Doria* in 1956.
3. Sorry—according to the Merchant Shipping Act 1995, you must report your find within 28 days or face a criminal charge.
4. True. Author Jules Verne, who also wrote *20,000 Leagues Under the Sea*, followed Wyss' Swiss Family Robinson in 1900 with a novel called *Second Fatherland*.
5. Canada.
6. *Gilligan's Island, Cast Away, Lost, Survivor, Mutiny on the Bounty, Lord of the Flies, Blue Lagoon* (to name a few!).

THE SHOW
Swiss Family Robinson

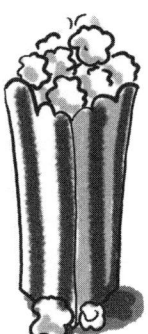

Genre: Family/Adventure

Length: 126 Minutes

Rating: G, although there are several scenes of action violence between pirates and the family. Very young children may also be frightened by a tiger and by a fight with a snake in the river.

Plot: The Robinsons, a family of five from Switzerland, are on their way to become part of a new settlement in New Guinea when they're shipwrecked on a deserted island. The resourceful family uses remains of the ship along with island debris to build a treehouse and the necessary tools to survive.

The two older of the three Robinson sons explore the island in order to find help, but along the way they discover pirates holding two British captives. The Robinson boys rescue one of the captives, a girl, and return with her to the family's treehouse. But problems arise when the two brothers compete for her affections. And, if that weren't enough, a lurking, deadly tiger continues to stalk the family and angry pirates want their captive back.

A battle ensues between the outnumbered Robinsons and their swashbuckling adversaries, when suddenly a ship appears on the horizon. Who has arrived to rescue the Robinsons? Will the family choose to leave their island paradise, or will they return to the civilization they once knew?

Bible Passages
You may want to use these Bible passages during your movie discussion:
- *Joshua 1:7-9—Be courageous.*
- *Ecclesiastes 4:9-12—There is power in teamwork.*
- *1 Thessalonians 4:11-12—Lead a quiet life.*

THE POST-SHOW

After the movie, use some or all of these questions to discuss the spiritual themes in *Swiss Family Robinson*.

 Each person in the Robinson family was important to the family's survival on the island. How are members of your own family important?

 When Fritz and Ernst left the treehouse to explore the island, their mother had to watch them go. How do you think the she felt, not knowing what was in store for her sons? What advice would you give her?

 Fritz and Ernst were close brothers and got along great together. What happened to change all of that? Tell about a time you were really jealous of someone close to you and how it affected your relationship.

 Which is best, to stay at home where we know we're safe or to venture into a dangerous world? Explain your answer.

Friendship, Faith, and Fun for Small Groups

 How can kids let their parents know when they're ready to face the world?

 Sometimes we worry about our lives instead of trusting God. In what areas do you need to trust God more? How can you give him your trust?

 The Robinson parents decided to remain on the island, where they felt they had everything they needed. Do you think you could be content on a desert island if you had your loved ones with you? Explain.

 What does it take to make you content? What keeps you from being content with what you have or where you are in life?

 A Swiss pastor wrote *The Swiss Family Robinson* in 1812 to teach about family values, the natural world, and self-reliance. What lessons can we learn from the movie about courage?

…about learning to be content?

…about teamwork?

PRAYER

End the evening by praying together. Ask for prayer requests. Encourage each person to share one specific way to put into practice the lessons learned from the movie *Swiss Family Robinson*. Have each person pray for someone else in the group; for example, everyone could pray for the person to the left.

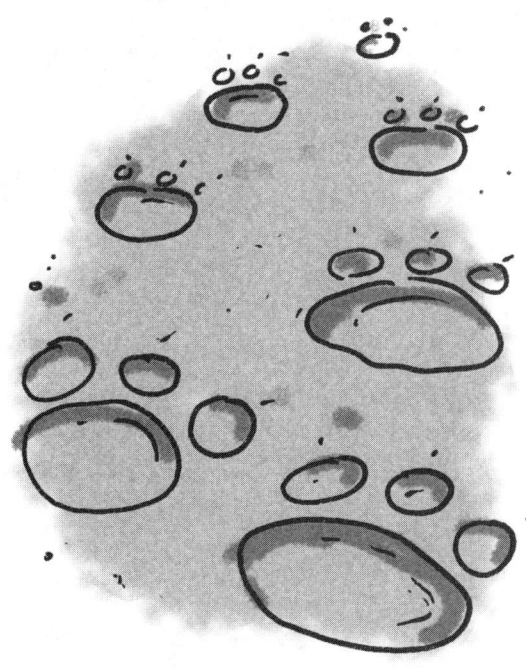

71

SUPPLIES

Before your Dinner and a Movie event, you may want to talk to everyone who plans to attend and divide up the ingredients list. Keep in mind that some items, such as the ground beef and wieners, may cost a lot more than others. Perhaps two people would like to share the cost of the meat, while others each bring a couple of items.

Easy Option Meal
Make this simple meal even easier by picking up hamburgers and hot dogs at a local fast-food restaurant before your guests arrive. Or, if you'd like to "switch hit" the menu, opt for fried chicken and potato salad instead. Just about anything that works for a tailgate gathering will work for this dinner and movie!

What you'll need:	Names:
Ballpark Burgers (serves 8)	
2 pounds ground beef	_____
1 package taco seasoning mix	_____
2 eggs	_____
1 cup crushed corn chips	_____
½ cup finely chopped onion	_____
8 hamburger buns	_____
Home-Run Hot Dogs	
1 wiener or sausage per person	_____
1 hot dog bun per person	_____
chips of your choice	_____
ketchup and mustard	_____
pickle relish or pickle slices	_____
onion slices	_____
tomato slices	_____
lettuce leaves	_____
Beverages	_____
1 store-bought ice-cream bar per person	_____
peanuts and popcorn	_____
Make Ahead **Line-Drive Lemonade (recipe on page 74)**	_____

Permission to photocopy this page from *Group's Dinner and a Movie: G-Rated* granted for local church use. Copyright © Group Publishing, Inc., P.O. Box 481, Loveland, CO 80539. www.group.com

GROUP'S DINNER AND A MOVIE: G-RATED

Set the Stage

Root for the home team! Before guests arrive, cut pennant shapes from white paper, and set these out with crayons or markers—everyone can decorate these in his or her favorite baseball team's colors as guests arrive. Hang these creations with clothespins on a cord stretched from wall to wall or within a door or window frame.

Print black-and-white pictures of past baseball greats from the Internet, then place these about the room along with bats, gloves, balls, and even uniforms if you have them. You might want to hang signs around to indicate locker rooms, the bench, the outfield, and other locations associated with a ballpark.

Much of The Rookie takes place on a small-town ball field, so your table setting should be as simple as a picnic or tailgate gathering. A bright tablecloth, paper plates, and cups are perfect! For added fun, purchase popcorn bags at your local paper and party goods store to serve snacks in during the movie.

And, if you want to score that extra run, try these ideas: Rent a popcorn or cotton candy machine from a local party rental place, continuously run a DVD of baseball bloopers until dinner starts, or print scripts from the Internet of Abbott and Costello's hilarious "Who's on First?" routine for guests to read aloud after the meal.

BALLPARK BURGERS

2 pounds ground beef	1 cup crushed corn chips
2 eggs	½ cup finely chopped onion
1 package taco seasoning mix	8 hamburger buns

Break the eggs into a ½ cup measure. Beat with fork and add water to fill. Crush chips in a bowl and add the eggs, onion, and taco seasoning. Let sit for 5 minutes. Mix with ground beef and form into 8 patties. Grill over medium heat for about 4 minutes on each side. Serves 8.

LINE-DRIVE LEMONADE

6 lemons	6 cups water
1 cup sugar	

Mix sugar with one cup of water in a small saucepan. Heat until sugar is completely dissolved. Meanwhile, squeeze lemons until you have about a cup of juice. Pour sugared water, lemon juice, and remaining 5 cups of water into a gallon pitcher, and chill. For a special touch, add a few lemon slices to the pitcher and serve over ice cubes made from lemonade. Makes about 2 quarts.

COOKING  TOGETHER

1. Just before guests arrive, prepare the grill.

2. Remind everyone of the importance of washing their hands before preparing a meal and after handling meat. Have an adult chop the onions. Have a couple of adults supervise kids as they create the egg mixture, crush the chips, and add them with the taco seasoning and onions to the hamburger meat according to the recipe above. The meat mixture will be heavy, so an adult will likely need to combine the ingredients by stirring with a wooden spoon or by hand. Kids can make the patties by forming on waxed paper and transferring to a platter to be brought to the grill.

3. As the host, assume grill duty—or ask a volunteer to cook the burgers and hot dogs while you coordinate the other kitchen activities.

Permission to photocopy this page from *Group's Dinner and a Movie: G-Rated* granted for local church use. Copyright © Group Publishing, Inc., P.O. Box 481, Loveland, CO 80539. www.group.com

4. Ask volunteers to separate hamburger and hot dog buns and arrange these on a paper plate or place in a wicker basket for the table.

5. Invite two kids to arrange sliced pickles, onions, tomatoes, and lettuce leaves on a serving plate.

6. Remaining volunteers can set the table, prepare beverages, and put out the ketchup, mustard, and chips.

7. Have everyone gather at the table. Ask someone to pray, then enjoy this tailgate-style meal!

8. Cleanup is easy! Put any leftovers in the refrigerator. Gather the used paper products, and place in a recycling bin or in the trash.

9. Set popcorn and peanuts in the room where you'll show the movie.

Meal Time TalkStarters

> • *If you could play any position on a major-league team, which position would you play? Why?*
> • *If you could take anyone to a baseball game with you, who would it be? Why?*
> • *Athletes work very hard to become successful. How is that like other hobbies or jobs? Give an example.*
> • *In what ways do you think life can be like a game of baseball?*

LET'S WATCH A MOVIE!
THE ROOKIE
THE PRE-SHOW

Have everyone gather in the area where you'll show the movie. If you've just finished eating dinner together, you may want to provide a quick break for people to use the restroom.

When everyone has gathered, serve Line-Drive Lemonade and ice-cream bars to anyone who's ready for dessert. Invite everyone to snack on peanuts and popcorn during the movie. Be sure to provide napkins and also paper bowls or cups for the snacks.

Have adults team up with kids in groups of three to five, and give each group a piece of paper and pen. Ask groups to answer these trivia questions about the game of baseball. Then read the answers aloud so all can compare their answers to the correct ones.

BASEBALL TRIVIA QUIZ

1. What was the first team to play baseball under modern rules?

2. When was the first World Series played? Who won?

3. True or false: Original baseball rules allowed a fielder to put a runner out by throwing the ball at him, but *only* if it hit him.

4. Who has the best lifetime batting average?

5. What pitcher holds the record for the most wins?

6. Who is the only pitcher to win the Rookie of the Year, Cy Young, and MVP awards?

7. What pitcher holds the record for the most strike-outs?

8. Who holds the record for the fastest pitch?

9. Extra points to the team that can sing "Take Me Out to the Ball Game."

Answers
1. The New York Knickerbockers (formed in 1845).
2. 1903—Boston won.
3. True (ouch!).
4. Ty Cobb (.366).
5. Cy Young (511 wins)—but he also holds the record for most losses!
6. Don Newcombe.
7. Nolan Ryan (5,714).
8. Nobody really knows, though most record books acknowledge Nolan Ryan at 100.9 mph in 1974. Since then, radars have clocked up to 103 mph, but Major League Baseball doesn't recognize radar speeds as an official statistic.

THE SHOW
The Rookie

Genre: Family/Biography

Length: 127 minutes

Rating: G

Plot: Dennis Quaid stars as Jimmy Morris in this true story about a baseball hopeful whose dreams of playing in the big leagues were dashed early on, then surprisingly resurrected years later.

As a child, Jimmy has a passion and a talent for baseball, but his father, a ranking official in the Navy, has no time to entertain Jimmy's dream of pitching in the World Series. That, coupled with the family's frequent moves to different states, prevents Jimmy from getting any farther than the minors before injuring his shoulder and giving up baseball. He marries and becomes a high-school science teacher and baseball coach in a small Texas town surrounded by oil rigs.

Hoping to motivate his players to improve their ballgame, Jimmy agrees to try out for the Tampa Devil Rays if the boys win their district championship. When they do win, Jimmy finds himself at the Devil Rays tryouts with his children in tow. His pitch is clocked at 98 miles per hour, and, despite his age, Jimmy is recruited to play for the professional team. With his dream finally realized, Jimmy has to decide how—or if—he can balance his love of baseball with his love for his family.

THE POST-SHOW

After the movie, use some or all of these questions to discuss the spiritual themes in *The Rookie*.

 Coach Morris told his high-school team, "If you don't have dreams, you don't have anything." Do you agree with him? Why or why not?

 What's your "big dream"? How will you make it come true?

 What discouraged Jimmy from following his dream of becoming a big-league pitcher? What makes you feel discouraged from reaching your dreams or goals?

 How was Jimmy's early relationship with his father different from his relationship with his own son? Why do you think Jimmy treated Hunter differently than he was treated as a boy?

 How can we bring out the best in our family members (parents, children, spouses)?

 After Jimmy reaches his dream of playing professionally, he discovers new problems. Have you ever thought reaching a goal would make life better and then found out it just created new problems? If so, share about that time and what you did to solve those problems.

 The real Jimmy Morris actually appears in *The Rookie* as an umpire at one of the games. How do you think it felt for him to have a movie made about his life? What kind of movie would be made about your life? Who would you like to star in that movie?

 Do you think a person is ever too old to reach for a new dream?

Bible Passages

You may want to use these Bible passages during your movie discussion:

- *Deuteronomy 5:16—Honor your parents.*
- *1 Samuel 16:7—God looks at the heart.*
- *Proverbs 14:23—Hard work brings profit.*
- *Jeremiah 29:11—God has good plans for you.*
- *Romans 8:28-29—God causes all things to work for our good.*

PRAYER

End the evening by praying together. Ask for prayer requests. Encourage each person to share one specific way to put into practice the lessons learned from the movie *The Rookie*. Have each person pray for someone else in the group; for example, everyone could pray for the person to the right.

SUPPLIES

Before your Dinner and a Movie event, you may want to talk to everyone who plans to attend and divide up the ingredients list. Keep in mind that some items may cost a lot more than others. Perhaps two people would like to share the cost of those items, while others each bring a couple of items.

What you'll need:	Names:
Spaghetti a la Robinson (serves 10)	
1½ pounds ground beef	_____
two 26-ounce jars spaghetti sauce	_____
Italian seasonings	_____
1 large onion, chopped	_____
2 cloves garlic, minced	_____
1 green pepper, chopped	_____
dry spaghetti	_____
butter	_____
Franny's Salad (serves 10)	
lettuce (one or more heads of your favorites)	_____
1 package frozen English peas	_____
1 medium purple onion	_____
2-3 stalks celery	_____
1 package dried cranberries	_____
croutons	_____
bottled salad dressing (your choice)	_____
Time Traveler's Bread (serves 12)	
1 loaf shepherd's bread	_____
1 loaf Italian bread	_____
butter or margarine	_____
garlic salt	_____
Frankie's Frog Concoction (makes 1½ quarts)	
lemon-lime soda or sparkling water	_____
sugar-free lemon-lime drink mix	_____
lime sherbet	_____
maraschino cherries	_____
Grandma Lucille's Chocolate Chip Cookies (recipe on page 81) *(Make Ahead)*	_____

Easy Option Meal

If your group isn't inclined to cook, pick up spaghetti to-go from your local Italian restaurant or deli—just heat and eat!

And Grandma Lucille won't mind if you purchase store-bought cookies or even use frozen cookie dough instead of her recipe. (Who is she?—You'll meet her in the movie.)

 Permission to photocopy this page from *Group's Dinner and a Movie: G-Rated* granted for local church use. Copyright © Group Publishing, Inc., P.O. Box 481, Loveland, CO 80539. www.group.com

GROUP'S DINNER AND A MOVIE: G-RATED

Set the Stage

Set out sheets of butcher paper or poster board along with crayons or markers. As guests arrive, ask them to imagine a crazy invention they'd like to make, and then have them draw their ideas on the paper provided. Encourage them to show lots of detail—including dimensions, if they can. Tape these to the walls of your dining area or TV room.

Use protractors, rulers, pencils, graph paper, notebooks, and other lab essentials as decorations for your table. For extra fun, purchase small plastic frogs from a party goods store and scatter them on the dining table, then let everyone take them home as souvenirs.

Because the movie has a futuristic motif, choose plastic or metallic-looking place settings for your table. For example, use clear plastic plates, cups, and flatware, and use aluminum foil wherever your imagination leads. If you have metal mixing bowls, use those to serve the spaghetti and salad in.

SPAGHETTI A LA ROBINSON

1½ pounds ground beef	2 cloves garlic, minced
two 26-ounce jars spaghetti sauce	1 green pepper, chopped
Italian seasonings	dry spaghetti
1 large onion, chopped	2 tablespoons butter

In a large size pot, brown meat until crumbly. Drain grease. Add the next five ingredients to the meat, simmering uncovered and stirring occasionally until sauce is heated through at desired consistency. Boil pasta according to package directions. Drain and stir butter into pasta to keep it from sticking together. Just before serving, either combine the sauce and pasta in one large bowl or serve the two in separate bowls. Serves 10.

FRANNY'S SALAD

lettuce (one or more heads of your favorites)	2-3 stalks celery
1 package frozen English peas	1 pkg. dried cranberries
1 medium purple onion	croutons
	bottled salad dressing (your choice)

Cook peas, then drain and rinse in cold water to chill. Wash and tear lettuce into bite-sized pieces. Quarter and slice onion and celery. Toss all with cranberries and croutons in a large bowl. Serves 10.

TIME TRAVELER'S BREAD

1 loaf shepherd's bread	butter or margarine
1 loaf Italian bread	garlic salt

Place the shepherd's bread on a serving plate. Cut the Italian loaf in half widthwise and set the halves on either side of the shepherd's bread; these will be "wings" attached to the shepherd's bread "fuselage." If necessary, carve the Italian loaf so the halves sit snuggly against the shepherd's bread. Serve butter and garlic salt on the side. Serves 12.

FRANKIE'S FROG CONCOCTION

1 liter bottle lemon-lime soda or sparkling water

1 package sugar-free lemon-lime drink mix

about 3 scoops of lime sherbet

1 cup maraschino cherries

In a large pitcher, combine lemon-lime soda or sparkling water with lemon-lime powdered drink mix. Stir in cherries. Just before serving, add a few scoops of lime sherbet. Makes about 1½ quarts.

GRANDMA LUCILLE'S CHOCOLATE CHIP COOKIES

1 cup butter or margarine, softened

¾ cup sugar

¾ cup packed brown sugar

2 eggs

1 teaspoon vanilla extract

2¼ cups all-purpose flour

1 teaspoon salt

1 teaspoon baking soda

12-ounce package semi-sweet chocolate pieces

Preheat oven to 375. Cream butter and sugars. Beat in eggs and vanilla. Add flour, salt, and baking soda until well mixed. Stir in chocolate pieces. Drop by rounded teaspoonfuls onto cookie sheet. Bake 10-12 minutes. Remove to cooling rack immediately. Makes about 2 dozen.

COOKING TOGETHER

1. When everyone arrives, remind children of the importance of washing their hands before preparing a meal. Ask two children to help an adult volunteer make Franny's Salad according to the recipe on page 80.

2. Have two adult volunteers prepare the spaghetti sauce and pasta according to the recipe on page 80.

3. Have a child and adult work together to create the Time Traveler's Bread according to the instructions on page 80.

Meal Time TalkStarters

• What invention are you most grateful for?

• Imagine you've just been given a huge science lab of your very own. What will you invent?

• Would you rather travel back in time or visit the future? Why?

• What would you change about your life if you could go back and have "do-overs"?

Permission to photocopy this page from *Group's Dinner and a Movie: G-Rated* granted for local church use. Copyright © Group Publishing, Inc., P.O. Box 481, Loveland, CO 80539. www.group.com

4. Have a couple of older kids prepare Frankie's Frog Concoction according to the recipe on page 81.

5. Have the remaining guests set the table and prepare dinner beverages.

6. Bring food to the table, and have everyone gather. Ask someone to pray over the meal. Then enjoy!

LET'S WATCH A MOVIE!

MEET THE ROBINSONS

THE PRE-SHOW

Have everyone gather in the area where you'll show the movie. If you've just finished eating, provide a quick break for people to use the restroom.

When everyone is together, serve Grandma Lucille's Chocolate Chip Cookies and Frankie's Frog Concoction to anyone who's ready for dessert.

Have adults team up with kids in groups of three to five, and give each group a piece of paper and pen. Ask groups to answer these trivia questions about time travel. Then read the answers aloud.

TIME TRAVEL TRIVIA QUIZ

1. Who is the crazy scientist in *Back to the Future?*

2. True or false: Albert Einstein believed time travel was possible.

3. In *Superman: The Movie*, how does Superman travel back in time?

4. In what movie does an angel take George Bailey to his past to see what the world would've been like if he'd never been born?

5. In the story *The Sword in the Stone*, a certain wizard can travel through time. What's his name?

6. Who tells Scrooge that he'll be visited by spirits who take him to the past and also to the future in *A Christmas Carol?*

Answers

1. Doctor Emmett Brown.
2. False. He believed time travel would require traveling faster than the speed of light, which he said was impossible.
3. He flies against the world's orbit, and makes the world turn in reverse, which turns time back.
4. *It's a Wonderful Life.*
5. Merlin.
6. The ghost of Jacob Marley, Scrooge's old partner.

THE SHOW
Meet the Robinsons

Genre: Family/Adventure

Length: 95 minutes

Rating: G

Plot: Based on the book *A Day With Wilbur Robinson* by William Joyce, this digitally animated adventure is about a boy-genius named Lewis. There's nothing ordinary about Lewis, and adoption interviews continually end in disaster as he tries to impress prospective parents with inventions that turn out to be rather…messy. Desperately wanting a family, he decides to find his real mother and works around the clock on his finest invention yet: the Memory Scanner. He's sure it'll help him remember what she looked like the last time he saw her.

But someone else wants Lewis' invention. At the school science fair, a mysterious villain named Bowler Hat Guy sabotages the invention. Before Lewis can even figure out what's happening and link the events together, he meets Wilbur, a strange boy who whisks him away in a time-travel machine to a dazzling city of the future. Lewis ends up at Wilbur's home, and though he tries to hide his futuristic family from Lewis (and Lewis from his family), their chance meetings finally culminate in an unveiling of the truth. Lewis learns that he has something spectacular to look forward to.

But what about Bowler Hat Guy? He's foiled, of course—but not before he unwittingly teaches us a lesson about revenge, forgiveness, and letting go of a hurtful past.

THE POST-SHOW

After the movie, use some or all of these questions to discuss the spiritual themes in *Meet the Robinsons*.

- Who was your favorite character? Why?

- Walt Disney said, "We keep moving forward, opening new doors and doing new things, because we're curious, and curiosity keeps leading us down new paths." What was Lewis curious about until the very end of the movie? Where did that curiosity lead him?

- The grown-up Lewis had the motto "Keep moving forward" for Inventco. If you had a motto for your life, what would it be?

- Wilbur's family was a little…strange! But they all loved each other in spite of being so different. How could Wilbur's family be a good example for you and your family?

Young Lewis was advised to let go of the past. Do you think that's a good idea? Why or why not?

 Who did Bowler Hat Guy blame for the way his life turned out? Do you agree with him? Explain.

Bible Passages
You may want to use these Bible passages during your movie discussion:

• Proverbs 17:17—A friend loves at all times.

• Jeremiah 29:11—God has good plans for you.

• Romans 8:28-29—God causes all things to work for our good.

• Galatians 6:9-10—Help those in God's family.

 What do you think happens to us when we focus on revenge instead of forgiveness or understanding?

 One of the songs from *Meet the Robinsons* is called "The Future Has Arrived." What do you think that means? How could things we do or say today impact our future?

 Lewis desperately wanted to be adopted, but then he gave up on that and desperately wanted to find his real mother. Since God already has plans for us, what could Lewis have done instead of worrying so much? In what areas of your life do you need to rely on God more?

 What can *Meet the Robinsons* teach us about being a good friend?

…about taking responsibility for our choices?

…about moving forward?

…about trusting God?

PRAYER

End the evening by praying together. Ask for prayer requests. Encourage each person to share one specific way to put into practice the lessons learned from the movie *Meet the Robinsons*. Have each person pray for someone else in the group; for example, everyone could pray for the person to the right.

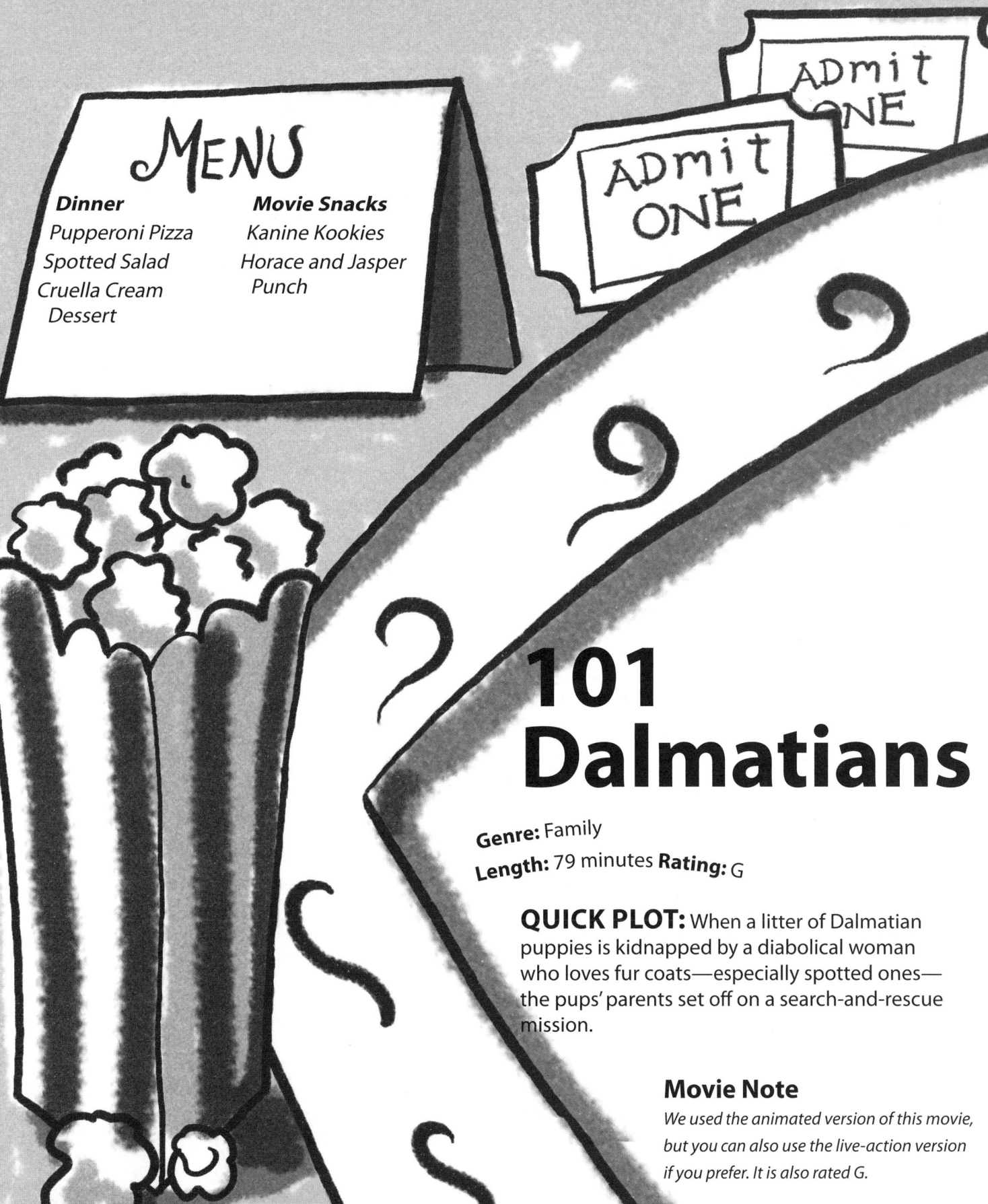

GROUP'S DINNER AND A MOVIE: G-RATED

Easy Option Meal

Is your time together limited, or you just don't feel like making a mess in the kitchen tonight? Call your local pizzeria and order a pepperoni pizza to-go. They'll even deliver the soda!

SUPPLIES

Before your Dinner and a Movie event, you may want to talk to everyone who plans to attend and divide up the ingredients list. Keep in mind that some items may cost a lot more than others. Perhaps two people would like to share the cost of those items, while others each bring a couple of items.

What you'll need: **Names:**

Pupperoni Pizza (makes 1 large pizza)

1 loaf frozen bread dough _____

1 jar pizza sauce _____

1 package pepperoni slices _____

8 ounces mozzarella cheese _____

Spotted Salad (serves 6-8)

1 head of lettuce _____

2 tomatoes _____

2 carrots _____

1 cucumber _____

1 can medium black olives _____

1 jar of salad dressing _____

Horace and Jasper Punch (makes about 1 gallon)

2 quarts lemonade _____

2 liters lemon-lime soda _____

Make Ahead **Cruella Cream Dessert (recipe on page 88)** _____

Make Ahead **Kanine Kookies (recipe on page 87)** _____

 Permission to photocopy this page from *Group's Dinner and a Movie: G-Rated* granted for local church use. Copyright © Group Publishing, Inc., P.O. Box 481, Loveland, CO 80539. www.group.com

86

Recipes

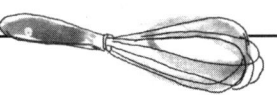

PUPPERONI PIZZA

- 1 loaf frozen bread dough
- 1 jar pizza sauce
- 1 package pepperoni slices
- 8 ounces mozzarella cheese, grated

Allow bread dough to thaw and rise.

TIP:

Be creative with your pizza ingredients! Any round-shaped topping such as black olives or sausage will fit the "spotted" theme of your gathering.

Preheat oven to 390 degrees.

Roll out dough into desired shape on either a cookie sheet or pizza stone. Pour pizza sauce on dough, and spread evenly over entire pizza, leaving ½ inch for crust. Evenly cover pizza with pepperoni slices then sprinkle with cheese.

Bake in oven at 390 for 10 minutes. Turn and bake an additional 5 minutes, or until cheese is melted and crust is brown. Makes 1 large pizza.

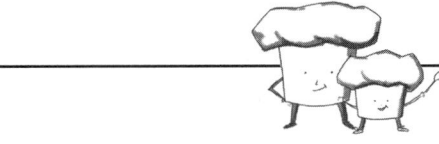

SPOTTED SALAD

- 1 head of lettuce, torn into bite-sized pieces
- 2 tomatoes, cubed
- 2 carrots, sliced
- 1 cucumber, sliced
- 1 can medium black olives, drained
- 1 jar salad dressing

Combine first five ingredients in a large bowl. Serve chilled with salad dressing.

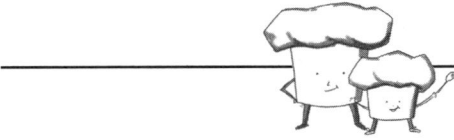

HORACE AND JASPER PUNCH

- 2 quarts lemonade
- 2 liters lemon-lime soda

For each glass of punch, combine ⅔ lemonade and ⅓ soda.

Make Ahead

KANINE KOOKIES

1 roll refrigerated sugar cookie dough

On a lightly floured surface, roll out dough to ¼-inch thickness. Using a small-sized round cookie cutter, cut out a circle to make the center of a dog's paw. Make four small balls, approximately ½ inch wide. Set in a row along the top of the cookie. Press gently to create the toes to resemble a dog's paw.

Bake at 350 for 12-15 minutes. Makes 2 dozen.

GROUP'S DINNER AND A MOVIE: G-RATED

Set the Stage

Decorations for this event are, of course, black and white!

Before your movie event, have your kids help cut paw prints from black poster board or construction paper. Arrange the paw prints in a path leading to your front door. Smaller paw prints can be used indoors, leading guests to rooms such as the kitchen, the dining room, the bathroom, and the room where the movie will be shown.

Hang large black and white construction-paper spots from the ceiling using string and tape—your guests will see spots before their eyes! And kids will enjoy bundles of black and white helium balloons placed about the rooms, especially if they can bring a balloon home as a souvenir.

For the dining room, use a white paper or plastic tablecloth to cover the table, and scatter black confetti or paper dots on top.

Are you willing to go that extra mile? Purchase small dog bowls at the local dollar store to serve your cookie snacks in.

CRUELLA CREAM DESSERT

1 package (8 ounces) cream cheese
1 package (3 ounces) cream cheese
1 cup confectioners' sugar
3½ cups cold milk
2 packages (1 ounce each) instant vanilla pudding mix
1 carton (12 ounces) whipped topping, thawed
1 package (18 ounces) cream-filled chocolate sandwich cookies, crushed

In a large mixing bowl, beat the cream cheese and confectioners' sugar until smooth. In a large bowl, whisk milk and pudding mixes for 2 minutes; let stand for 2 minutes or until soft-set. Gradually stir into the cream cheese mixture. Fold in the whipped topping.

Spread 1 ⅓ cups of crushed cookies into an ungreased 13x9x2-inch pan. Layer with half of the pudding mixture and half of the remaining crushed cookies. Repeat layers. Refrigerate for at least 1 hour before serving. Serves 10-12.

COOKING TOGETHER

1. Before everyone arrives, thaw the frozen bread dough and let it rise according to package directions. Each loaf will make one large pizza.

2. When guests arrive, remind them of the importance of washing their hands before preparing a meal. Have a small group of kids work with a couple of adults to make Pupperoni Pizza according to the recipe on page 87. Let each child have a turn rolling as many thawed loaves as needed into the shapes of pizza.

3. When pizza is formed, have kids spread the sauce over the dough, leaving approximately ½ inch around the edge for the crust.

4. Ask a child to peel apart the pepperoni slices and place them evenly over the pizza while an adult grates the mozzarella cheese. When the pepperoni is in place, let kids sprinkle the cheese on top. Place the pizza in the oven.

5. While the pizza is baking, ask for several volunteers to tear the lettuce for the salad and place in a large serving bowl. Have adults chop the vegetables, and have kids sprinkle these ingredients over the greens. Chill the salad until dinnertime.

6. Ask an adult and child volunteer to prepare the Horace and Jasper Punch according to the recipe on page 87.

7. Have others set the table and pour beverages.

8. Have everyone gather at the table. Ask someone to pray over the meal. Then enjoy the pizza!

9. Bring out the Kanine Kookies to serve during the movie. See recipe on page 87.

> **Meal Time TalkStarters**
>
> • Tell about a favorite pet you had or knew when you were a child. What made this pet so special?
> • Why do you think some pet owners treat their pets like people?
> • How do pets bring comfort to people?
> • What's the most mischievous thing your pet—or a pet you know—has ever done?
> • What's the strangest or funniest pet story you've ever heard?

THE PRE-SHOW

Have everyone gather in the area where you'll show the movie. If you've just finished eating dinner together, you may want to provide a quick break for people to use the restroom.

When everyone is together, serve Kanine Kookies along with Jasper and Horace Punch to anyone who's ready for snacks.

Have adults team up with kids in groups of three to five, and give each group a piece of paper and pen. Ask groups to answer these trivia questions about dogs. Then read the answers aloud so all can compare their answers to the correct ones.

DOGS TRIVIA QUIZ

1. What country used to worship dogs as though they were gods?

2. Why were poodles originally bred?

3. In laboratory tests, which prove to be smarter: dogs or cats?

4. Based on a dog's average lifespan of 11 years, how much does it ultimately cost to own one?

5. What color are Dalmatian puppies at birth?

6. Why are Dalmatians often associated with fire stations?

7. According to a book of records, what is the heaviest and largest dog?

8. What is the smallest dog?

9. Name three cartoon characters that are dogs.

Answers

1. Egypt.
2. To be hunting dogs.
3. Dogs are far superior, especially in problem-solving and learning commands.
4. About $8,000.
5. White—their spots appear a bit later.
6. Before automobiles, firemen relied on horse-drawn coaches to get them to the fire. Unfortunately, horse theft was a real problem, so they used Dalmatians to guard against thieves because Dalmatians are fiercely protective of horses. From then on, they've been mascots of firehouses.
7. In 1989, an Old English Mastiff was recorded as weighing 343 pounds and measuring over 8 feet long from nose to tail.
8. In 1945, a Yorkshire Terrier was recorded as weighing only 4 ounces and measuring 3½ inches from nose to tail.
9. Pluto, Scooby-Do, Snoopy, and Clifford, to name a few (what kind of animal was Goofy, exactly?).

THE SHOW
101 Dalmatians

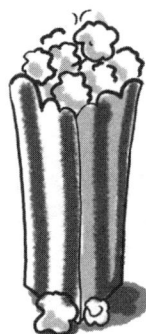

Genre: Family

Length: 79 minutes

Rating: G (Young children may find certain scenes and characters to be scary. For example, Horace and Jasper must break into a home to steal the puppies in one scene, and in another the two chase the puppies in an attempt to capture them. And Cruella De Vil is…well…not a nice person.)

Plot: Roger, a bachelor composer who lives alone in a messy apartment, has only his devoted Dalmatian named Pongo to keep him company. But though Roger is quite content with the bachelor life, Pongo is ready for companionship. One day, while looking out the window of their apartment, Pongo spies a beautiful female Dalmatian with her owner heading toward the park. Suddenly in the mood for a walk, Pongo leads Roger to the park, where they just happen to run into the dog Perdita and her owner, Anita.

It's not long before Roger and Anita are married and Pongo and Perdita are expecting a litter of puppies. Life is wonderful—that is, until Anita's former schoolmate comes to visit. Cruella De Vil (who, incidentally, has a passion for fur coats), is a rather unpleasant guest who's suspiciously interested in the arrival of the puppies.

No sooner are the puppies born than Cruella insists on buying them from Anita and Roger, but Roger refuses, and Cruella's greedy plans are thwarted. Infuriated, she hires thugs Jasper and Horace to abduct the puppies from their home. Pongo and Perdita are heartbroken when they discover that their pups are missing, but information from the "dog network" leads them to the old De Vil home where the precious puppies are held captive. How can they rescue their little Dalmatians before Cruella wears a new black-and-white coat?

THE POST-SHOW

After the movie, use some or all of these questions to discuss the spiritual themes in *101 Dalmatians*.

 What was your favorite part of the movie or your favorite character in the movie? Why?

 How did other dogs help Pongo and Perdita in their time of need? How can you encourage others during difficult times?

 Cruella told Anita: "My only true love, darling. I live for furs. I worship furs! After all, is there a woman in all this wretched world who doesn't?" What are some material things that we tend to worship without realizing it?

 The Bible tells us to be on our guard against greed. How can another person's greed hurt us? How can our own greed hurt us?

 How would you describe Cruella? Do you think it would be hard to forgive her if she'd stolen something from you? How do you think forgiveness could affect someone like her?

 Anita was always kind to Cruella. What does it mean to "do to others what you would have them do to you" (Matthew 7:12) when the "others" are people you don't like?

 How can you show God's love to someone who's hurt you?

 What does this movie teach us about how to treat our friends?
...our family?
...our enemies?

Bible Passages
You may want to use these Bible passages during your movie discussion:
- *Matthew 7:12—Treat others as yourself.*
- *Luke 12:15—Beware of greed.*
- *Ephesians 4:32—Be kind and forgiving to each other.*
- *1 John 3:17-18—Help others in need.*

PRAYER

End the evening by praying together. Ask for prayer requests. Encourage each person to share one specific way to put into practice the lessons learned from the movie *101 Dalmatians*. Have each person pray for someone else in the group; for example, everyone could pray for the person to the right.

Come Join us for Dinner and a Movie: G-Rated

We'll watch

The Rookie

and enjoy a tailgate-style meal!

When: _____
Time: _____
Where: _____
_____
_____
RSVP: _____

Come Join us for Dinner and a Movie: G-Rated

We'll watch

FINDING NEMO

and enjoy scrumptious sea fare!

When: _____
Time: _____
Where: _____
_____
_____
RSVP: _____

Come Join us for Dinner and a Movie: G-Rated

We'll watch

MARY POPPINS

and enjoy a traditional London feast!

When: _____
Time: _____
Where: _____
_____
_____
RSVP: _____

Come Join us for Dinner and a Movie: G-Rated

We'll watch

Chicken Run

and enjoy finger-lickin' chicken!

When: _____
Time: _____
Where: _____
_____
_____
RSVP: _____

Cut the invitations along dashed lines.

Permission to photocopy this page from *Group's Dinner and a Movie* granted for local church use. Copyright © Group Publishing Inc., Box 481, Loveland, CO 80539. www.group.com

Come Join us for Dinner and a Movie: G-Rated

We'll watch
WILLY WONKA AND THE CHOCOLATE FACTORY

and enjoy hearty home-style cooking!

When: _____
Time: _____
Where: _____
_____
_____

RSVP: _____

Come Join us for Dinner and a Movie: G-Rated

We'll watch
101 DALMATIANS

and enjoy delicious Pupperoni Pizza!

When: _____
Time: _____
Where: _____
_____
_____

RSVP: _____

Come Join us for Dinner and a Movie: G-Rated

We'll watch
Charlotte's Web

and enjoy a barnyard banquet!

When: _____
Time: _____
Where: _____
_____
_____

RSVP: _____

Come Join us for Dinner and a Movie: G-Rated

We'll watch
Meet the Robinsons

and enjoy a Robinson family dinner!

When: _____
Time: _____
Where: _____
_____
_____

RSVP: _____

Cut the invitations along dashed lines.

Permission to photocopy this page from *Group's Dinner and a Movie* granted for local church use. Copyright © Group Publishing Inc., Box 481, Loveland, CO 80539. www.group.com

Come Join us for Dinner and a Movie: G-Rated

We'll watch

Cars

and enjoy a feast for the racetrack!

When: _____
Time: _____
Where: _____
_____
_____
RSVP: _____

Come Join us for Dinner and a Movie: G-Rated

We'll watch

Swiss Family Robinson

and enjoy a tropical feast!

When: _____
Time: _____
Where: _____
_____
_____
RSVP: _____

Come Join us for Dinner and a Movie: G-Rated

We'll watch

The Wizard of Oz

and enjoy an over-the-rainbow buffet!

When: _____
Time: _____
Where: _____
_____
_____
RSVP: _____

Come Join us for Dinner and a Movie: G-Rated

We'll watch

The Sound of Music

and eat a few of Maria's favorite things!

When: _____
Time: _____
Where: _____
_____
_____
RSVP: _____

Cut the invitations along dashed lines.

Permission to photocopy this page from *Group's Dinner and a Movie* granted for local church use. Copyright © Group Publishing Inc., Box 481, Loveland, CO 80539. www.group.com